Barging into France

Gerard Morgan-Grenville

Barging into France

Illustrated by the author

David & Charles : Newton Abbot

ISBN 0 7153 5456 6

Set in 11 on 13pt Baskerville
and printed in Great Britain
by W J Holman Limited Dawlish
for David & Charles (Publishers) Limited
South Devon House Newton Abbot Devon

Contents

Illustrations

I am sure I would rather be a bargee
than occupy any position under Heaven
that required attendance at an office...
So far as I can make out, time
stands as nearly still with him as is
compatible with the return of bedtime
or the dinner-hour. It is not easy to
see why a bargee should ever die.

Robert Louis Stevenson

Foreword

This book, besides being an account of the adventures and misadventures of a barge, the *Virginia Anne*, is intended to convey an impression of life on the continental waterways and to say something about the rivers and canals of Holland, Belgium and France and the local characteristics peculiar to each.

Any such journey is of necessity a personal affair, with tempo and mood dictated by the barge herself, so I have not portrayed in any detail the crews who hazarded their fortunes to those of the *Virginia Anne*.

No attempt has been made to provide a continuous travelogue as such. Information and history of the regions and towns encountered are freely available from the local tourist offices. But I have allowed myself some purely subjective digression in an effort to provide the reader with a clue to the reason for my being, first, a continental bargee and only second an English citizen.

If the reader is tempted to follow suit, I should like to address to him a solemn plea. Most of the waterways he will encounter are currently well maintained, relatively unpolluted and staffed and used by a generous and friendly fraternity—even if one or two of the exceptions to this last have been singled out for comment in the narrative which follows. It took me time to learn the respect which I now have for these conditions. My plea is that, before you go, you acquaint yourself with the rules: do not abuse the freedom given to you, jettison nothing imperishable or poisonous into the water, and do not forget, *'toujours la politesse'*.

If I seem patronising, I ask your indulgence for although the English have a good name at present, I have recently seen a few who have shown a thoughtless and even a blatant disrespect for these principles.

I have avoided the temptation of dedicating this book to my wife, my secretary, my crew or even to some resplendent, but alas fictitious, Italian princess, so that I may be free to place the dedication where in all truth it properly belongs.

So, to the *batellerie* of France, who with patience, humour and constant kindness have enabled me to pursue my wanderings and indulge my enthusiasms—to these *brave hommes* for whom a barge provides a hard-found living, I dedicate this book.

Burgate House   Gerard Morgan-Grenville
Godalming   1971

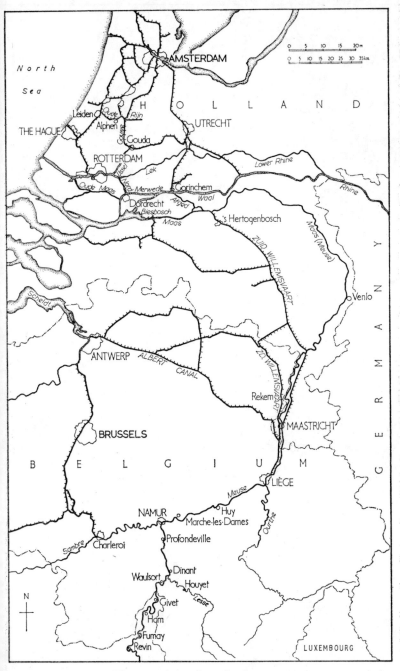

First section of author's route

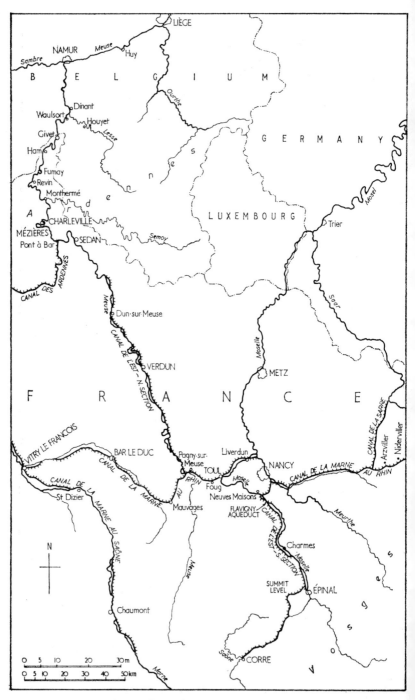

Second section of author's route

I

Preliminary rumblings

Looking back, I think the foundations of what was to become an obsession were laid that afternoon.

The drive to Pisa airport had been conducted in an atmosphere of mounting panic. A last swim in the Mediterranean intended to cool us against the heat of travel on a stifling September's afternoon had achieved the opposite effect. We had as usual stayed too long. Even the reckless Italians seemed to be driving ralentissimo as I urged our feeble hireling to greater speed. Near the perimeter of the airfield we took a wrong turning. 'Ask the way!' we both said together and as always, as if at some secret prearranged signal, every human being vanished. Turning and backing with rising temperature, we found the way through the labyrinth of sordid tenement blocks that only the Italians seem able to dispose around their cities with such abandon and such unerring ugliness.

Our thirteen pieces of luggage, ten of them hopefully classified by us as 'light hand-baggage for use on the flight', became an immediate embarrassment. We had overdone it this time and the charge of excess baggage placed on our faces that stamp of gloom that so often distinguishes the returning holidaymaker.

The sun did its best to make a final mockery of our cooling bathe as we walked across the shimmering concrete of the airport apron. Clutched firmly under my right arm was an extremely large black leather portfolio containing the result of two weeks' hard labour—five oil paintings on nineteen square feet of assorted canvasses. I was greatly concerned to see that the still wet paintings travelled unmolested. In their interest I decided to abandon the usual struggle for a window seat and dropped to the tail of the queue. Just inside the aircraft door I saw the Alitalia steward and, summoning a look of authority which was intended to forestall argument, handed him the precious portfolio.

'Please look after these carefully and see that no-one bumps into them.'

'Sorry, Signor, no room.'

'You *must* have room. B.E.A. always have room,' I said, hoping to catch his competitive spirit.

'Sorry, Signor, it should have been with the registered baggage. Too big for cabin. Much too big.'

'Will you give it to the pilot to look after then. He's got plenty of room.'

'Impossible! Impossible, Signor! The pilot, he take nothing, Signor.'

'Put it on a spare seat then—they are paintings,' I added in some desperation, appealing to the artistic sense said to be latent in all Italians.

'There are no spare seats, Signor. You must place them under your seat.' He disappeared behind a curtain and I took it that the subject was dismissed.

I moved up the aircraft to the remaining seat and attempted to carry out the suggested operation. It was quite impossible. Apologising to my neighbours, I sat with the immense case on my knees, largely obscuring all forward vision. I could feel numerous pairs of dark Italian eyes boring into the back of my neck with annoyance at this stupid *Inglese* with his outsize portfolio.

As the aircraft banked and climbed over the coast, I had a brief glimpse of the place where a short while ago we had so pointlessly bathed: the thin strip of dirty hotels, each with room-with-own-bathroom-balcony-and-view-of-sea, distinguished from each other only by their grandiose names. Concealed beneath the canopy of umbrella-pines, the close-packed alabaster souvenir shops, the *gelati* men, the dust, noise, heat and the whole apparatus of world tourism stretching like an endless ribbon into the merciful blue haze.

The aircraft levelled out and the view changed to the far-off hills of Tuscany which we had left the same morning. The swiftness of transition irked me as it always does and I began to reflect for the hundredth time on the shortcomings of all forms of modern travel. Now I had the added complication of transporting half a hundredweight of painting gear and I was beginning to understand why artists are seldom patrons of the airlines. My wife and I had already discarded the motor-car as an acceptable form of transport; the cramped, claustrophobic interior filled so often with the obnoxious fumes of other vehicles, one of a solid echelon of cars crawling along an endlessly twisting road. Railways have always seemed a poor compromise, combining many of the worst features of other forms of travel; on the Continent more particularly, the austerity of the timetables, the lack of directional freedom—not to mention the difficulty and expense of stopping on impulse to inspect more closely some exciting architectural or natural feature—all made an alternative means of travel preferable.

I was just beginning to reflect that the next holiday was going to need some original planning when my neighbours

B

started to lower their tables in anticipation of a meal. They seemed to be as fascinated as I was to know what I proposed to do. My table was separated from me by the wall of canvasses on my knee. I could sense that any effort I made to resolve my difficulty was likely to be to the entertainment of all. I decided to get rid of the portfolio without delay and by now was prepared to trust its treatment to luck. I turned it round so that it trespassed as far as possible into the gangway. The stewardess came up and with feline grace glided straight past it. I eased it out further. Out of the corner of my eye I saw the steward approaching.

'Would you like me to take your case, Signor?'...

In April earlier that same year, I was standing at the railway ticket-office waiting to hear by how much the price of a ticket to London had increased that week and reading a copy of *The Times* further up the queue. My eye was caught by a three-line advertisement beginning 'DOR-DOGNE—barn for sale'. That particular region in the south-west of France has long held a special fascination for me. With its peaceful rivers and wooded hills, its ancient villages and ruined castles, I think of it as the embodiment of rural France. The thought of buying an old barn there in some peaceful corner and slowly converting it for our part-time habitation had seldom been far from mind.

As soon as I read the advertisement I knew that yet another journey would originate from the famous Personal Column. By the time the train reached London I had completed, as I believed, a masterly design for the interior. I wrote to the advertiser. He sent me a blurred photograph of an indeterminate farm building. But, in case of disappointment, I wrote to all the local estate agents, made

The barn 'held together with lichen'

appointments and drove out in the first week of May.

Spring had hardly started in England when I left, yet here it was in full swing. The flowers appeared in ever greater profusion as I descended the narrow wooded valley to the barn. Suddenly I caught sight of it high above the road behind a rocky outcrop. I scrambled up the steep bank, the scent of lavender and thyme heavy in the air. Rock-roses, grape-hyacinths and narcissi competed for space between the rocks.

It was a beautiful barn with a golden lichen on the old stone walls. Lizards scurried into cracks. Chaffinches sang in a lilac dense with flower. Further down the hill a stream made summery noises over rounded stones. For several minutes I sat quite still, hypnotised by the sudden enchantment, not daring to move lest the spell be shattered. Then, imperceptibly, dawned the realisation that it was only the golden lichen that kept the barn together at all. Conversion would be quite impractical.

I spent three days visiting countless barns, abandoned farms and village cottages. Something of Arcadia was common to them all. Yet gradually the feeling developed: with so much of Europe still to see, did we yet want to put down roots and return each time to the same place? As my objection grew, so the house agents waxed ever more eloquent in praise of their properties. But I left them to their lively imaginations in which all their barns boasted a *'vue panoramique'* and all their pig-sties *'tout confort'* and headed north again.

It was midsummer a year or two before and we were sitting in a partly mown hay-field by the side of the river Lot. We were drying in the beating sun after a bathe in the earthy waters. It was early afternoon and no-one stirred. Only the faintest breath of air rustled the highest leaves of the alders lining the banks. We sat there with half-closed eyes, the thousand scents of hay suspended in the haze.

'*Bonjour M'sieurdame!*' We looked up, startled. A gnarled hand touched a stubbly chin in salutation. A large straw hat pushed to the back of his dusty head, an old farmer shuffled towards us.

'*Venez au bistro?*' he enquired somewhat incongruously. Ignoring a mumbled reply, he approached the water's edge and slowly bent down. We watched in fascination as he started pulling a string attached to a low branch. He must, we thought, have lured a fish with infinite cunning to some primitive trap whilst he attended to the haymaking. Suddenly it appeared—a large bottle of red wine.

'*Vous avez soif?*' he asked, as in one fluent movement he extracted glasses from beneath the leaves of a huge burdock and filled them.

We drank the wine, joined the farmer and his family in haymaking, bathed again and drank more wine. The last shafts of sun filled with the crooked flight of insects. The cool dark river-smell invaded the hay-field. A faraway tractor was bringing home the final hay-load of the day.

We climbed back into the hot, stuffy car and started the evening search for a room. Anxious to preserve liberty of movement, we never booked rooms in advance and on this occasion it was not until we had enquired at five hotels that we found a room. Weariness added to the sense of anti-climax; a perfect day had ended in the discordant quest for accommodation. By the time we were installed in an airless, noisy hotel room, we were no longer in the mood for the kind of meal to which we had been looking forward earlier. This dependence on hotels and the constant unpacking and repacking of suitcases was becoming increasingly tedious.

I had no doubt that, however keen the traveller, there

were tiresome problems which could only detract from the potential enjoyment. But the reflection proved a mental cul-de-sac: so long as one travelled one was bound to remain subject to the limitations of established forms of transport and accommodation. I thought back briefly to days when I had walked with a tent on my back. But although I had certainly enjoyed independence, it was just about all I had enjoyed. I was not a natural member of the thick-legged brotherhood that strides doggedly along the roadside verge in rain or sun alike.

One winter's day I was driving home from the office when without warning the idea came to me. *The thing I most needed was a motorised barge.* Of course! The more I explored the idea, the more certain I became that it was right. At first I turned it over lightly, idly ruminating on the possibilities, much as one might taste a new wine. Then, for all the world as though the wine contained a powerful drug, it began to take hold of me and by the time the car was in the garage I knew that there was no going back. After all, it provided answers to all my problems.

Simultaneously it combined all the advantages of a house with those of a mobile studio, a constantly changing scene before its windows. It offered complete independence of cars, aeroplanes, trains and hotels and an end to living out of suitcases. We should be able to travel in comfort and at our own leisurely pace. We should be able to sail regardless through forests, valleys, fields and towns, step ashore and wander where we wished, and all without so much as leaving home.

It never occurred to me in the first flush of excitement that my wife might not think it quite so splendid an idea.

But fortunately my enthusiasm seemed to communicate itself to her and she at once agreed. I sat down and wrote to the editor of every paper and magazine to do with boats. I wrote to all the larger boatyards. I wrote to every name listed in the London telephone directory under Barge, Boat, Marine, Sea, Ship and Yacht.

Within a few days stones were turned and avenues explored. A pattern began to develop. The world of those who prefer water to dry land is divided into two. There is the world of the ship, sea-going and professional, a closed order strictly for the dedicated. Then there is the world of the yacht with its rigorous social strata—at one end the dinghy owner and at the other the Riviera motor-yacht magnate; both have in common a language and an overcommitment of time and money, but little else. Somewhere between these two worlds lies the *demi-monde* of the bargee. He and his craft are curiosities of a bygone age.

Correspondence with boatyards ceased on the instant as soon as the point was driven home that it really *was* a barge I wanted. After all, why should their commercial interest be aroused by anything so outmoded? The entire weight of their salesmanship is absorbed by commercially viable boats, pleasure-cruisers, yachts, real ships that take to the open sea. A barge is an anachronism, a dying species fit only for the graveyard; but only in England, and then only as a result of the lack of interest in the British canal system shown by successive governments. Nowhere else in western Europe are the canals as neglected as in Britain. For at the very time when the rest of the canalised countries of Europe were planning vast expansion and modernisation programmes, in the 1880s, Britain chose to let hers stagnate, throwing in her entire lot with the developing railways. She pays for it today, of course, by having no cheap bulk-transport system for raw materials and in the unnecessary overcrowding on her roads.

My barge was to be used for exploring the Continent, I had decided. If I purchased it in England, I should have to sail it across the Channel. Most of the surviving English barges were no longer enjoying bow-to-stern health and the prospect of a Channel crossing inspired few of my friends to volunteer for the journey. But one was prepared to try with a barge that he had located. This was one of the last of the Thames sailing-barges, the *Veronica*, then lying at Greenhithe. We visited her one foggy day; her still white hull, the name painted in red and gold lettering, gave a romantic break to the endless vista of mud and slime of the Thames estuary. Never having had anything to do with sailing, I was cynical of boat-lore and the whole business conjured up an image of some gloom. So far I had been indulging in harmless daydreams and now I wondered whether the reality might not expose my mistake. Yet as I climbed out of the deep hull of the *Veronica* I suddenly saw the point. Or rather I felt it, and I knew that boats had entered my life. Sadly we left her to the rising tide; she was just too wide for the canals of Europe.

I saw one other sailing-barge still complete with masts and lee-boards. She had been converted below deck into a warren of windowless rooms. She was filthy and her great timbers were being allowed to rot for lack of care. Finally I saw another ancient canal-barge which until recently had been drawn by horse for the haulage of planks. But she was too small and I realised that I should have to continue the search abroad.

I heard from one firm that there were for sale in Holland three barges of the type and size that conformed to the specification I had given. A few days later I learned that one of the three had been sold and another withdrawn. I received a photograph of the third and knew at once that I *must* have it. It had already been converted and was the right size. It would be an almost exact fit in some of the locks and under some of the bridges in France, but it was not actually too large. The writer of the accompanying letter added mysteriously that his firm's activities had nothing to do with the sale of boats but that he had obtained the information from other sources and hoped that he was being of assistance.

It was then to this firm's office in Maastraat, Rotterdam, that I now hurriedly set forth one day in January in a state of considerable anxiety lest 'my' boat should have been sold.

2

Love at first sight

It had been a restless night in which confused dreams had alternated with attempts to master the fierce heat of the radiators. The Rotterdam hotel in which I had arrived the previous evening had not been constructed for Englishmen, for the windows were designed so as not to open more than an inch or two. The dry air parched my throat and I was first down to breakfast. My urgent pleadings for coffee went unheeded for an age. Then suddenly breakfast appeared. My clamour had evidently been interpreted as a sign of acute hunger; beef, ham, cheese and black bread were added to the usual breakfast menu. But not coffee.

Finally, well fortified, I left the hotel. I was far too preoccupied to take other than a passing interest in my surroundings. Nevertheless, looking back, it occurs to me that there have been changes since Lady Mary Wortley Montagu visited the city in 1716. For it was Rotterdam that she described in a letter home as being 'so neatly kept that, I will assure you, I walked almost all over the town yesterday, incognita, in my slippers, without receiving one spot of dirt'.

As for me, I had not ventured out in my slippers and should not have favoured my chances if I had. A few small snowflakes were drifting fast across the square and a biting wind chased litter through the herds of cyclists. The already drawn faces in the tram queues stared unseeing through the struggling traffic. Holding the lapels of my overcoat close about my neck, I hurried toward Maastraat, wondering whether it would be as I had pictured it each time I had addressed a letter there: a long, low quay beside the river Maas; the tall, narrow windows of a classic Dutch façade overlooking a crowded waterway. The climax to those weeks of anticipation was approaching.

Maastraat was a disappointment. The Maas was nowhere in sight and the featureless grey houses were enlivened only by the shining brass plates of numerous businesses. I pressed the bell at the enquiry desk and waited. A girl came.

'May I help you?' she asked in English, using the sixth sense that all foreigners seem to possess to enable them to determine nationality unerringly.

'Mr Overberg please.'

'I'm sorry, Sir. Mr Overberg is not here.' She seemed glad that she could not be of assistance.

'But I have an appointment with him,' pulling his last letter from my pocket.

'I'm sorry, Sir. Mr Overberg is not with the business any longer. He left yesterday and he is not coming back.'

The temperature of the already stuffy office climbed several degrees. Had my whole journey then been in vain?

'May I see the person who has taken over from Mr Overberg then?'

'I'm sorry, Sir, but no one has come to take his place yet.' She was a negative girl whose point in life was probably to prove everything impossible and whose happiness depended on the discomfiture of her victims.

'I'd like to see the manager then,' I said, a trifle loudly.

She disappeared, no doubt hoping to return in triumph with the news that the manager was busy. But no, almost at once he appeared. He listened to my story with sympathy and surprise; evidently he had not known that he was temporarily in the shipbroking business. He rummaged amongst some files on the unfortunate Mr Overberg's desk. It was all there—all the information and the address of the caretaker who lived next to the boat's mooring. I was bowed out into the freezing street.

My next appointment was with a surveyor. I hurried round to his office. We got into his car and drove straight round to the address I had been given.

I saw the barge at least a mile before we reached her. She was moored on a canal high above the surrounding land. Like much of the rest of Holland, this part between Rotterdam and Amsterdam should rightly be at the bottom of the sea. But it is reclaimed land, with only the canals at sealevel. Power-driven pumps replace the old windmills and maintain the water level which stops only just short of the top of the dykes. Thus from a long way off I could see the barge in her entirety, looking for all the world as though some giant hand were lifting her.

We collected the caretaker. As we walked along the raised canal bank, the cutting edge of the wind was quite unblunted. But there she was! She was a beautiful boat and she seemed to radiate a kind of peaceful timelessness. Any lingering doubts that there may have been in my mind suddenly vanished. I walked up the plank and went over her above and below in a kind of trance. The surveyor crawled unhappily through the bilges holding a lighted candle. Emerging on deck, he aimed a kick at the wheel-

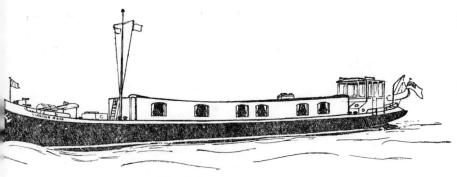

mv Virginia Anne

house; clearly he was not in love with her. I enquired anxiously as to the soundness of the wooden hull. 'It's not wooden,' he corrected, with some astonishment. 'She's built of iron.' I had not noticed.

I was given the address of the owner at The Hague. An hour later I arrived and, with a hollow stomach, paused momentarily before pressing the bell. The owner was a lady of great charm who spoke fluent English. From the first it seemed decided that I was to have the boat and the possibility of my not wanting her did not even enter into it. The owner had recently been widowed and was about to part with the boat, sadly, after sixteen years. She and her husband had converted her after the war. Before that she had plied up and down the Maas carrying sand for the estuary dykes since 1912, the year of her birth.

We agreed to visit the barge the next day and I returned to Rotterdam for a second sleepless night.

Early the following morning I caught the train to The Hague. It was during this journey that one of those little incidents occurred that seem often to determine the trend of events for the day. I have a horror of being climbed over by other people's children and therefore became most depressed when two women and three babies got in and arranged themselves around me; within seconds I was being pawed and pulled while the women smiled indulgently at their enterprising offspring. A few minutes later we arrived at Delft station and I turned to watch the platform scene. The train re-started and I looked round again. The women and babies had vanished. A remarkably pretty girl was sitting opposite me. The omens for the day were good!

There was no feeling of anticlimax on this second visit. The black-tarred hull looked somehow unreal as she lay moored in her elevated position on the canal, taking the full blast of the icy winds. The water had frozen over during the night and the white superstructure all but merged into the mist beyond.

The temperature inside the saloon was a cool four degrees below freezing but hot coffee was produced and conversations resumed, interrupted every few minutes by a visit to some new part of the boat. With each exploratory journey fresh possibilities emerged and the excitement was extreme. There was that distinctive smell throughout: a compound of tar, floor polish and bilge water, with occasional overtones of oil and paint. This smell has since become a source of acute nostalgia; I have only to come across something that reminds me of it and I am instantly aboard.

Perhaps at this point I should give some facts about the vessel which at this moment represented the focal point of my universe. If subsequently this subject of my dreams was to become the theatre of sudden nightmares, it in no way detracts from my memory of the first full exploration I made of the frozen interior.

The length of the barge is almost 100 feet—well over that of three London Transport buses stood nose to tail; the beam measures some 15 feet and she draws just under 5 feet. Already a formidable bulk for anyone who has driven nothing larger than a motor car, the great length makes any sideways manoeuvre in a narrow cut a near impossibility. From the detachment of an armchair, the dimensions had been mere figures. I had to see the barge for myself and stand over the wheel-house controls to grasp just what I was taking on. Built before World War I when the fashion in barges was for bows more pointed and sterns more rounded than those of today, the *Virginia Anne* progresses with a minimum of wash.

Climbing down a steep stairway (or companionway as I think of it now) from the foredeck, one finds oneself in the fo'c'sle, a triangular space lined with lockers and cupboards and with a fireplace at the apex of the triangle. Cupboard doors on either side of the companion way open up into two minute cabins. The area is lit by portholes and a large rounded roof light. A water-tight steel bulkhead isolates the fo'c'sle from the rest of the boat as a precaution against collision flooding. These fifty odd square feet made up the entire living accommodation of the bargee families who sailed her in her professional cargo-carrying days before her conversion; families of five or six frequently existed all their working lives in space that now provides cramped sleeping quarters for two of our three children. Bargee families today have a little more room, but living space can only be gained at the expense of the hold, and cargo is money.

Behind the fo'c'sle is a large hold with doors to the bilges which run back as far as the engine-room bulkhead near the stern. A passage runs from the hold along the port side as far as the saloon. The first door leading from the passage connects with a double cabin and the next with a W.C. The door beyond that leads into the main bedroom, a largish room with twin beds, hanging cupboard and one of the longer walls entirely fitted with drawers and cupboards. A bathroom leads off the bedroom; it actually does contain a bath, besides a W.C. and washbasin. Another door from the bedroom leads into the saloon which spans the width of the ship. Here too, as along the length of the passage, all the walls below window height are lined with built-in drawers and cupboards occupying the space below the gangways. All the windows are large and slide fully open, affording not only a superb panorama of the passing scene but marvellous ventilation in the summer heat. The saloon and passage are panelled throughout in a light wood. An oil-fired stove heats the saloon, the hot-water system and the central-heating system. From the saloon a door connects with the hall, which is entered from outside by means of a large hatchway and a flight of steps leading up to the level of the deck. A door off the hall leads into the kitchen (or galley), itself connected by a hatch to the saloon.

From the deck two hatches give access to the engine-room, which is separated from the living accommodation by two water tanks extending the width of the boat and containing over thirteen hundred gallons. The water in the lower of these two tanks is electrically pumped into the upper.

The engine-room, which features from time to time in this narrative, contains—apart from the main engine—an auxiliary generator, a 300 gallon oil tank, a fitted workshop bench, a timber store, pumps, switchboard, fuel drums, tools and a huge assortment of gear, spares and various boxes containing a miscellany of objects, many of which remain unidentified to this day.

Above the engine-room is the wheel-house. Apart from a comfortable bench and a table occupying half the space, the rest of the room is kept free of obstacles in order to maintain adequate freedom for the often panic-driven rotation of the huge wooden wheel. The view from this elevated position is superb. A control panel to one side of the wheel contains the various engine gauges, switches and levers, the speed indicator, gas detector, depth sounder, clock, compass and the master unit for the loud hailer and cabin intercommunication system.

I have described the barge as it is in its present form. At the time of my visit it lacked proper cooking and heating facilities and the sanitary arrangements were unmistakably continental. There was only a modicum of control and navigating equipment. A nearby shipyard carried out the modifications. The engine with which the barge was fitted was an 80 horse-power, pre-World War II American petrol engine, and although I looked upon it with much suspicion I decided that it would nonetheless have to stay; a replacement would be unthinkably expensive.

If the impression gained from this factual description is one of luxury, then I should quickly reassure my reader that, with the exception of the navigating equipment— and this for reasons that will become apparent—none of the fittings is of the type to be found on smart yachts. The impression should rather be one of solidity and functional utility, though I will not pretend that in such circumstances it is not possible to live in great comfort. If comfortable but unsmart within, the observer has only to look at the exterior to know that this is neither Cowes nor Cannes.

And so it was that I completed my first examination of the barge that morning. In spite of the hot coffee, we were utterly frozen and we hurried to a nearby restaurant to be revived with Dutch gin. By the end of lunch all arrangements had been concluded and by mutual agreement we dispensed with the normal legal formalities and decided to draw up our own document of sale. Accordingly we sent for paper, carbon sheets and stamps and there and then drew up our Bill of Sale, much enjoying the saving of the sub-

C

stantial legal fees normally incurred in such transactions.

The barge was mine. Just what I had purchased I was none too certain. Never previously having owned or sailed a boat of any kind, I had no idea of the nature of my acquisition. In basic terms it seemed to be a powered houseboat capable in theory at least of navigation within the Western European waterway network. But whether it would actually move under its own power I did not know for certain. The engine had been dismantled for the winter as a precaution against frost damage and to have assembled it for a trial run would have necessitated spending more time than I could afford.

On my return journey to England I asked myself many times whether I had been the victim of *la forza del destino* or whether I had simply been carried away by an excess of enthusiasm. I suspected the latter. However, I was now committed and the exact nature of my purchase was to be revealed to me by stages.

3

Fuel to the fire

We spent our spare time throughout the rest of January and February collecting stores for the ship. The house was ransacked and gradually purged of anything that could be considered a duplicate. Visits to London for the Boat Show and the sales were followed by expeditions to ships' chandlers. Advertisements for strange but apparently indispensible pieces of equipment filled the yachting press; occasional orders were placed and soon there was a great fall-out of parcels. Everything was piled into one room and the job of packing started. Wooden crates and stacks of wood wool were procured and the packing room, normally the spare bedroom, began to look like a deep litter house for chickens. Shreds of wood wool found their way into every room in the house. Eventually the crates were nailed down, the words 'VIRGINIA ANNE' stencilled across them and some measure of sanity returned.

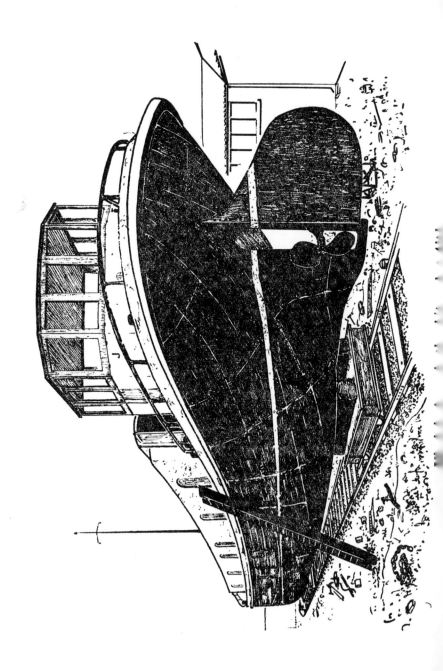

Choosing the name for the barge had not been easy. It was of course already named by its Dutch owner but the name was meaningless to us and indeed, as we later discovered, without meaning in Dutch. A change of name was therefore required and we anticipated no difficulty in finding an entirely suitable one. However, I soon found that all the names that occurred to us were already in use elsewhere amongst the world's shipping. Words with double meanings or particular connotations appeared briefly to be extremely funny, but the humour generally faded overnight.

In desperation I turned to the names of the vessels sailed by a 16th century ancestor, Sir Richard Grenville. The first had been 'Moonshine' and I wondered in passing whether with the passage of time he had tired of this witticism. The next was 'Castle of Comfort'; this seemed to offer too great a temptation to fate and was also dismissed. The last, 'The Virgin, God Save Her!' seemed more appropriate to the robustness of the humour of the first Elizabethan era than of the second.

Symbols and ideograms discarded, I resolved to simulate English bargees who, during the heyday of the barge at the end of the last century, frequently named their craft after their wives. Accordingly with a well-rehearsed spontaneity I made this touching proposal to my wife who was suitably gratified.

We had intended to take the crates with us in the guard's van of the train taking us to Harwich. However, enquiry revealed that the charges made by British Railways for the carriage of luggage in the luggage compartment of a train are so exorbitant that it was actually cheaper to hire a carrier to make the special 200 mile journey, thus helping to explain why the roads are full of lorries and the train luggage compartments almost empty.

As the carrier disappeared down the drive with his load of nine large crates, chest of drawers, ironing board and mini-bicycle, the project seemed really to be taking shape. Three days later, in mid-March, we set off. My wife was unable to come on the commissioning voyage and the crew consisted initially of three: my father as engineer, a neighbouring cowman as deckhand and myself. None of us had ever sailed anything and we were all totally ignorant of seamanship. Even the following ominous warning by a competent authority on the subject failed to undermine confidence: 'Sailing the seas is frequently child's play compared with navigating rivers.' I was subsequently to treat it with the respect it deserved. Nevertheless, on the eve of departure two concessions to professionalism had been made. A copy of a Nautical Almanack had been procured and a yachting neighbour had been called over to give a lesson on clove hitches and bowlines, both allegedly indispensible knots.

We practised these two curiously elusive knots until it was time to leave for the train. We then drew a sketch of them and hurried to the station with a practice length of rope. We found an empty compartment and with increasing frustration tried to master the trick. I proffered my wrist as a bollard; the slipping rope started to remove the skin. I offered my foot; the knot held but it was the wrong sort and it took some minutes to extricate my shoe. After half an hour of this we seemed to have achieved mastery over the clove hitch, although subsequent events proved otherwise. We moved on to the bowline and chorused the mnemonic 'the rabbit comes out of its hole, goes round the back of the tree and back into the hole'. It seemed so simple, yet the rabbit had a habit of re-entering the wrong hole. A variation in which a frog comes out of a pond was tried, but this only resulted in the manufacture of a splendid noose with a running knot. Holding this up for inspection in an effort to discover the error of our ways, we suddenly became aware of a figure standing in the doorway. A woman was staring at the noose, apparently transfixed with fear. After a few seconds of frozen horror, she fled to another carriage. On arriving at Harwich we discovered that our efforts with the rope had kept for us an empty compartment in an otherwise crowded train.

We filled in the time before departure in reading the Nautical Almanack. It seemed only prudent to learn the international emergency flag signals in case we should find ourselves out of control. All we really wanted was something like 'Please keep out of my way; I don't think I can stop', but this eventuality is apparently considered insufficiently feasible to be given reference, except in the full code book which we did not possess. The selection of messages might have been chosen by a compiler of foreign phrase books, so improbable did they seem, and we decided to commit only two to memory. The first was intended for normal use and as an insurance in case of collision: 'Although my ship is moving forward, my engines are going full speed astern'. We never discovered whether this in fact meant: 'My propeller seems to have been fitted back to front.' The second signal would be useful in discouraging contact with over-interested officials: 'I have a case of illness aboard and there has been unusually high mortality amongst the rats in the bilges.' It had never previously occurred to me that there might be rats in the bilges and whenever I have since had to visit them I have done so armed with a torch, a heavy stick and the greatest misgivings.

The ferry made the Hook of Holland at dawn. The previous day had been unusually fine and warm for the time of year and it looked as though the weather might be set fair for a period. This hope, however, was soon doomed to fade as the weather deteriorated steadily for eight consecutive days and provided conditions that we had not anticipated even in our most dispirited moments. The rowdy passengers of the night before tumbled out of the ship looking the worse for duty-free alcohol and gloomily lined the customs hall to answer the usual questions. Gradually the suitcases disappeared with their owners. My nine crates, chest of drawers, ironing board and mini-cycle became the centre of interest to the now unoccupied customs officials. After establishing ownership, the officials started to look over the crates in a most unhurried manner. At length the most senior of them came and asked for the second time:

'These all your bags?'

'Yes.'

'Ach!'

'May I clear them please?'

'Just a moment, I will find somebody.'

'Somebody' was not in a hurry to finish his breakfast, but eventually appeared with the first man.

'Are these all your bags?'

'Yes.'

'Ach!'

'May I clear them please?'

'Just a minute. I will fetch the officer.'

But it was still a little early for the 'officer'. The other officials faded away and the first man leant against the crates trying to give the impression that it would not be worth our while trying conclusions with him. The second man wandered in and out of the hall at intervals and eventually returned with the 'officer'.

'Do these all belong to you?'

'Yes, and I wish to clear them without further delay.'

'You cannot clear them.'

'I don't understand.'

'At the Hook of Holland you can clear only hand-luggage and vehicles.'

I insisted. 'But of course I must clear them. I have arrived with them. What do you suggest I do?'

'Ship them to Rotterdam or Amsterdam. Or send them by train. But they will have to be put in bond, you understand, and that is quite expensive.'

'How long will that take?' I was stunned.

'Two or three days, perhaps more,' he added brightly.

I felt trapped. The other officials reappeared in anticipation of a little unexpected drama. Something desperate was needed.

'I am not satisfied. I wish to speak to the chief customs officer immediately.'

'He has not come in.'

'Please find him at once. If you can't, I shall have to telephone the Chief of Customs at Rotterdam and the British Embassy in The Hague.'

'Perhaps he is in the canteen. I will see if he can come.'

His pace had noticeably quickened. The others tried to appear unconcerned.

'This way please.' The 'officer' beckoned me to a side door.

The chief customs officer was a tiny man who sat behind his desk in a self-important attitude, visibly grateful to his peaked cap for the effect of the extra inch or two it gave him. He wiped the corner of his mouth with a handkerchief, folded it with immense deliberation and replaced it carefully in his pocket. Then he looked up.

'So! You vish to see me?' Porcine eyes glared from his red face.

'I wish to clear my baggage immediately.'

'Your papers!' I thrust the copies of the packing list into his outstretched hand.

'So!' He appeared to study the contents with great care.

'Ach! So it is all personal baggage? You do not bring anything new?'

'That's right. All old stuff,' I agreed with an ingratiating smile.

'Vot about ze box of soap tablets? No new? Ach?'

'Quite right, quite right,' I said, forcing a laugh. He looked triumphant and treated himself to several moments' exultation.

'So! You vish to clear your baggage?' he asked again with sarcasm.

'Yes.'

A carefully calculated dramatic pause. Then

'Good. Everything is arranged.'

And he brought a rubber stamp crashing down on to the papers.

This sudden volte-face was evidently intended to represent a traumatic experience for the nearly-convicted smuggler.

'Thank you,' I said in as steady a voice as I could muster.

The cap was removed, replaced. He stood up and sat down again.

'You may go.'

'Thank you,' I said, feeling not unlike a boy emerging from the head-master's study.

The first obstacle over, the nine crates, chest of drawers, ironing board and mini-cycle were loaded into a waiting lorry. By the time we were ready to start the journey to the yard at Alphen-an-den-Rijn, some 30 miles north-east of Rotterdam, where the alterations had been carried out, the weather had already forgotten its early promise and a steady drizzle added to the man-made ugliness that characterises those areas of Holland below sea level. Nothing succeeds in relieving the dreariness of the rectilinear landscape. Even the occasional flash of carmine and yellow from the endless acres of greenhouses serves only to arouse sympathy for the plight of the helpless tulips within.

If Alphen's fame has spread beyond the Dutch borders, it is on account of its unlikely choice as the site of an aviary housing birds from all the corners of the earth. But that morning my thoughts were on the *Virginia Anne*. Would everything be ready or would we find that work had been held up due to lack of some vital part?

We saw her at once, moored at the far side of some barges. An assortment of people were climbing over her. I scrambled over the intervening barges to board her. She was larger than I remembered and the prospect of setting sail filled me with momentary anxiety. I went below and made a quick inspection. The damage done by the workmen was not irreparable and everything was more or less as I had remembered it.

The owner of the yard appeared and I braced myself to hear the customary tale of woe at the completion of any work. I determined to ask the question before he told me. Was everything ready? Yes, yes indeed, everything was completed. Was I satisfied? He very much hoped that I should find all to my satisfaction. Well of course if everything worked and if all the work had in fact been carried out according to his estimate, then I should certainly be highly satisfied; was this the case? Yes, yes indeed, but great difficulties of delivery had been met and only just overcome; the things ordered had just not come; alternative equipment had had to be obtained. The only trouble was that it had been necessary to pay rather more. . . The snag at last. Explained in detail, it might have been worse and I breathed a sigh of limited relief.

Meanwhile work had stopped in the yard and all eyes were focused on the newcomers. The lorry had arrived and was being unloaded. The mini-cycle made its appearance and provided the first visible proof of the strangeness of foreigners. It had grown colder and a wind was beginning to make the drizzle decidedly unpleasant.

Evidently the first thing to do was to change out of the clothes in which we had travelled. Although our attire had not been far above the minimum standard encountered on the ferry, here we felt like Paris models at a village fête. The crates were manhandled across two intervening barges, not without incident, and lowered into the hold for unpacking in the dry. Gradually the ship filled with more and more people.

The proprietor of the yard was beginning to warm up to the matter of his account and I was anxious to see exactly how well everything worked before taking too close an interest in what appeared to be a document of remarkable length. The heating engineers were taking the opportunity to tighten some of the pipes that had hitherto escaped their attention and the vendor of the oil-fired cooker was eager to have someone sign the acceptance form. Two customs officers appeared and for an unpleasant moment I felt that their visit must be connected with the incident at the Hook of Holland earlier that morning. However their only official interest was in duty on our Swedish-made refrigerator. The late owner of the barge, who had very kindly met us at the ferry, now returned with formidable quantities of stores of a consumable and largely liquid kind and was threading her way in and out of the kitchen between customs officers, engineers and workmen. Up on deck an elderly bargee was holding an old motor tyre in one hand and a length of rope in the other, eager to perform some service on my behalf; there was a hole in the surface of the tyre which he kept stabbing with the end of the rope, following this movement with a fluent twirling of the fingers, a look of great anxiety on his face. I finally understood that he wished to manufacture a fender for the side of the barge and required a

44

directive as to which type of knot he should employ. So already the Captain was being asked to demonstrate his mastery of Seamanship! Clove hitch or bowline? Surely it must be a bowline, possibly the classic example of the proper use of this knot, yet possibly quite unsuitable. How was one to tell? I was beginning to harden decisively in favour of the bowline when a bargee stepped briskly across, snatched both tyre and rope and proceeded to make a knot of astonishing complexity which ended in the requirement for a splicing tool. I slunk off, making a mental note that decisions of this kind must be made with lightning rapidity.

Peering down the hatch into the engine-room, I could see my father already engrossed with the health of some small part, spanner and rag in hand. Another man had appeared with a length of hose and was filling the water tanks. Our deck-hand was climbing across the other barges with jerry-cans of petrol. I returned below, determined to see how many people I could politely eject. Finding the customs men passing the time of day with the heating engineer, I had just decided to break up this meeting when pandemonium broke out on deck. The air was filled with shouts and guttural oaths. I made for the exit and prepared a dignified captainlike appearance guaranteed to forestall panic. But the yard owner brushed past me down the stairs shouting at the heating engineer who dropped the tools of his trade on the foot of the customs officer and dived behind the central-heating stove, which he extinguished instantly. I asked the nature of the crisis. As he scrambled toward the door, the yard owner shouted that one of the Englishmen had poured petrol into the diesel tank and that if this reached the oil-burning equipment the ship would explode. He was already on deck again making fast toward the quay. I thought I ought to mention this turn of events to my father in the engine-room; he was sufficiently interested to emerge from his lair with a minimum of delay. Our deck-hand was staring unbelievingly at the hole into which he had just poured the petrol. Everyone else had left the ship as with one well-drilled movement.

It was then that I remembered the appropriate flag signal: 'My ship is about to explode; please keep to a distance of more than five hundred yards.' But the flags were not yet unpacked from their locker and I was again frustrated in my efforts to demonstrate my professionalism. Captains went down with their ships, but were they expected to go up? I was not sure but compromised by going sideways onto the quay before my freedom of choice was removed.

There was still a great murmur of indignation in the yard. No doubt this sort of thing was only to be expected of people who rode miniature bicycles. At length it was agreed to telephone for a professional opinion as to the danger. A chemical engineer was prepared to state categorically that twenty litres of petrol in five hundred of diesel would not cause an explosion. The incident had cleared the boat of all supernumerary crew. Only the yard owner made a re-appearance, doubly anxious to re-open the matter of his account.

Left to sort out an indescribable muddle, the hours passed rapidly. By the time it had begun to grow dark we had unpacked most of the crates and found a home for all the larger objects. We had also taken mental stock of the ship's equipment, though there were vast gaps in our knowledge of the use of much of it. During the afternoon I had spent a few minutes in the wheel-house trying to accustom myself to the idea of steering this great length of ship along the narrow canals. The barge seemed to grow ever longer and it was hard to imagine that any control could be brought to bear on the bow so far away in front from a position at the

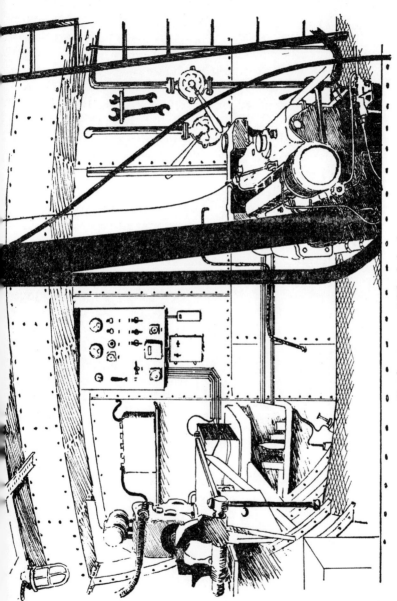

Engine room of Virginia Anne

stern. I tried turning the wheel. It was not easy. It measured some four feet across and required several turns to move the rudder through a significant arc. Steering alone was clearly going to call for considerable physical exertion.

My brief visit to the wheel-house increased my feelings of apprehension and I wondered momentarily whether it might be prudent to look around for a retired barge skipper who could give a few days' instruction. But this idea, though probably sensible, was patently defeatist and I did not want to be deprived at the eleventh hour of the experience which I had been eagerly anticipating for so long. Tomorrow, I thought, we will sail, regardless of the consequences.

In the warmth of the saloon and fortified by a toast in Dutch gin, the decision to sail without an experienced skipper seemed not unreasonable. After all, if we seemed to be heading for trouble, we could always stop. Or so I thought, and a second and third toast confirmed me in my view. I was intoxicated not so much by the alcohol as by the prospect of gliding gently along some peaceful canal in the warmth of a first spring day. And why not? It might well dawn warm and clear. A meal of unsophisticated simplicity was prepared from the contents of a tin of bully-beef. But the occasion lent it a rare flavour and the gaseous Dutch beer which washed it down might have been great wine. Replete and excited, we retired to our beds and slept the sleep of innocents.

4

Concession to the professional

The gentle rocking motion caused by the wake of a passing barge stirred me to consciousness. It was seven and time to be up. But it felt cold and the challenge ahead seemed infinitely more formidable in the light of day. I drew the curtains and surveyed the scene. One thing was certain: it was not going to be a warm spring day. The sky was grey, that particular tone of grey that comes with a wind of considerable coldness. A pennant flying from a barge moored at the other side of the canal was fluttering vigorously. The weather was continuing to deteriorate.

Breakfast was a failure. There was no milk for the coffee and we could not find the bread. A huge barge passed by only a few feet away; it seemed to occupy the whole canal and the prospect of competing for space with something of this size heightened the general feeling of unspoken apprehension. I emerged on deck. It was as cold as it had looked, but the wind was even stronger than I had feared. The barge next to us was loading with steel sheets and the flexing of the sheets as they were lowered into the iron hull made a dull thundering sound. The crew was just finishing loading one stack and paused before tackling the next. Their attention was caught by the *Virginia Anne* and one came toward me.

'You go today?' he asked in English.

'Perhaps,' I answered non-committally, not wishing to tempt fate further than necessary.

'You speak English?' I asked, suspecting that his opening remark represented the larger part of his knowledge of the language.

'The war,' he replied and left it at that.

Swallowing my pride, I decided to solicit advice and asked him whether the route I planned for the first part of the journey was in his opinion the best. He repeated my question in Dutch to the others, whereupon there was general laughter.

'De vay you go, you go good vor tventy kilometres, ven you no go more. De sluis not so big as de ship,' and he made expansive movements with his arms to indicate relative sizes. I was appalled. I had taken a lot of advice about the route and had confirmation that the locks were adequately large.

'Would you show me a better way if I fetch a map?' I asked.

He was delighted; obviously no-one had had recourse to his expertise for some time and the opportunity to demonstrate this and his English simultaneously was a rare stroke of luck.

I followed the meanderings of the black, stubby finger across the map. Every so often he would stop and jab his finger into it: 'Achtung! Danger! Big danger!' But he never knew the English for the particular type of danger and the Dutch meant nothing to me.

I concluded this meeting with the added worry that, as none of us spoke one word of Dutch, we were unlikely to know the nature of these danger points until they were actually upon us. The former owner was making her way across the yard with more stores and I explained my worries. It would be madness not to have an interpreter. Wait a minute! She knew 'just the person', a Dutchman who worked for the English Merchant Navy as a chief engineer, now retired and living in Amsterdam. Although the man was not on the telephone, he could sometimes be contacted through a nearby tobacconist. The tobacconist was rung. Incredibly our man was actually entering the shop to buy cigarettes. He agreed to catch the next train from Amsterdam. It seemed at the time to be a remarkably lucky coincidence.

We felt that the addition of this experienced seaman to our crew removed all remaining doubts about our ability to cope with all that lay before. We should leave just as soon as he arrived.

The red Ensign was unpacked and duly hoisted with appropriate ceremony. The ropes were made ready and on the side of the boat, away from the scrutiny of the other bargees, various attempts were made to apply clove hitches to the ship's bollards. Some worked, some didn't. We waited. We thought of trying the engine; it started instantly and appeared to run quite smoothly. We stopped it and waited again. We started the generator and made sure that the batteries were fully charged. We pumped the bilges until they were dry and still waited. We became convinced, in our impatience, that we could have managed quite well without any further help.

Finally a bus passed the entrance to the shipyard and some minutes later we were joined by an elderly man with a black homburg pulled down over the tops of his ears and without luggage of any kind. The arrival of the fourth member of our crew was taken as the signal to move. It was a tense moment. It was not until some time after we had set sail that we had an opportunity to find out about the professional seaman-interpreter whom we had so blindly signed on for a week.

5

A button marked 'START'

Four months had elapsed since I had given birth to the idea. I had at the outset small concept of the administrative effort required to launch it. In the intervening period of gestation I had written some two hundred letters to organise the modifications to the barge, secure equipment and fittings and obtain the necessary permits and certificates. Now all this was behind me. I was standing in the wheel-house with my finger poised over a large black button marked 'START'.

I looked quickly round to make sure that our professional seaman was still below; I had no wish to find my position compromised at this vital moment. My father shouted up from the engine-room that all was ready. Reaching for the megaphone, I gave instructions to the deck-hand to be ready to cast off. Then I pressed the black button. For some seconds I could only hear the starter labouring with decreasing enthusiasm in its effort to start the motor. Then suddenly it started and I yelled to the deck-hand to let go the ropes. I pushed the huge gear lever into the forward position. The engine slowed considerably and emitted a range of metallic sounds before settling down to the job of moving the boat. It was totally unsuccessful. I began to think that we must be secured to the quay, but no. More engine seemed to be the answer and I cautiously advanced the throttle lever a few notches. The engine responded with a new assortment of noises, but despite a great commotion in the water on one side of the ship beneath the wheel-house, I had only to look at the next-door barge to know that we were still not moving. My attention was finally attracted by my boatman friend of the morning pointing at something on the deck behind the wheel-house and then at the rudder. I saw that immediately above the rudder quadrant was a metal pointer which presumably indicated the direction of the rudder, the rudder itself of course being invisible from the wheel-house. It was pointing straight out over the canal at right-angles to the axis of the barge. What must have been happening was that the propeller was simply pushing us sideways into the adjacent barge. I spun the wheel as quickly as I could and waited for the results. They were electric.

We grated along the side of the next barge, a practice not much encouraged to judge by the expression on the bargee's face. We had pulled up the motor-car tyre fenders before leaving and now, realising our mistake, managed to insert one toward the stern. As the bow moved out, this fender took the entire strain for a brief moment before the rope broke and the tyre sank. Needless to say, it was the special fender made for us the day before.

The boat was crossing over to the other side at a frightening speed. Spinning the wheel in the opposite direction seemed to make not the slightest difference. I myself was still a safe distance from the opposite bank and reasonably unconcerned, but it did appear that the bow over which I was supposed to exercise at least nominal control was getting dangerously near. I swung the wheel further and threw the gear lever into neutral. After a while I did notice a slight tendency for the bow to move in the right direction, though plainly it was being subjected to far too little influence. I turned the wheel as far as it would go with all the strength I could muster; the bow took notice and swung round toward midchannel. Collision with the opposite bank at least was a danger of the past. For a short-lived moment I felt that we should soon be on course straight up the centre of the canal. A cruelly short-lived moment. For the bow continued to swing and no effect was apparent when I moved the rudder in the opposite direction. Now we were heading for the boat-yard. I set to work furiously on the wheel again and sent it spinning as though it were an old steam-roller wheel. After the proverbial eternity the bow responded sluggishly and we scraped along the far end of the boat-yard quay. I just had time to see two figures standing on the edge: the yard owner with a look of undisguised relief—his account having been settled—and the previous owner of our ship, her face buried in her hands.

Dimly grasping the problem of delayed-action steering, this time I started making alterations to the wheel considerably earlier, with the result that we avoided a frontal assault on the opposite bank and approached it at an altogether less steep angle. We made another less violent turn and gradually our snake-like progress resolved itself into a series of minor curves. After five minutes of frenzied activity behind the wheel I was exhausted. We had made almost no progress because the rudder had been hard over first one way and then the other. But we had covered a few hundred yards; the journey *had* started. During those first five anxious minutes fate had been good to us, for no other barges had wished to pass.

Perhaps the undulations were caused by insufficient steerage speed, so I experimented by opening the throttle still further. The noise level and vibration increased alarmingly with an occasional extra loud thud. Deciding that the fuller throttle positions were best left for emergency use only, I reduced the setting.

Meanwhile two things happened which were not easily ignored. Firstly the canal suddenly narrowed to about half width, making it difficult to see how two barges could pass. Secondly, the fourth member of the crew made his appearance on deck and entered the wheel-house. He was wearing my overcoat, pointing out by way of explanation that he had left his own behind. I was glad that he had been below during our departure. Although after the first few minutes I had recovered some much-needed confidence, this was now all sapped by the presence at my elbow of a genuine mariner. Worse even, we rounded a gentle corner and there, about half a mile ahead, was a bridge. It had two arches and I wondered which to take; the one on the left was substantially larger, yet a traffic signal instructed us to keep to the right. I sought my first piece of professional advice.

'What bridge?' asked the seaman.

'There, right ahead.'

'I can't see any bridge.' And indeed he couldn't.

This was our first clue that he might not be the asset we had hoped. Very early on he was christened Charlie. This for a number of reasons, one being that his own name was quite unpronounceable and indeed appeared never to be pronounced the same way twice. Charlie was a man of few words and when not otherwise engaged he would stand motionless in the wheel-house in a kind of trance, hands thrust deep in the pockets of my overcoat, his homburg pulled down over his ears, the stub of a damp, green cigar drooping from his mouth, staring far out in front with unseeing eyes. From time to time he would grunt, but we came to the conclusion that he must have been saying something in Dutch. He roused himself to action only when it was time to eat or when there was a crisis. In either event he reacted in a totally unpredictable manner.

The canal we were on was the Oude Rijn and, as in the case of many of the Dutch canals, it is not easy to state its terminal points; they are mostly links in the huge network of navigable waterways which range in every size from the huge Rhine estuary—navigable to vessels of several thousand tons—to the small drainage canals used by barges with a capacity as low as 40 tons. Just to our west lay Leiden, famous not only as the birthplace of Rembrandt but, I fear appropriately, also for its associations with the Pilgrim Fathers, for it was here that they lived for eleven years before setting sail in 1620 for America. The Oude Rijn will accommodate vessels of up to 1,000 tons.

But the canal narrowed still further. From the corner of my eye I could see the façades of some seventeenth and eighteenth century houses but, much as I should have liked to turn and study them, I was mesmerised by the spectre of the bridge in front. We were now only about a quarter of a mile from it—an awkwardly short distance in terms of our powers to stop—and a bend at the far side made it impossible to see if anything was coming. I decided to go through the larger of the two spans and risk something coming the other way. From a distance the bridge had looked high enough, but as we came nearer I felt less sure. About 200 yards away I knew that we should hit it. I decided to stop and heaved the gear lever into the astern position. We moved forward exactly as before. I opened the throttle full and, against the ensuing roar of disapproval from the engine, measured the speed of our progress against the bubbles on the water. If we were slowing at all, it was only very slightly and there was obviously no hope whatever of stopping before the bridge.

'A bridge! A bridge!' cried Charlie, making a wild pass at the gear lever. 'Full astern, quick!' he ordered, wrestling with the lever until he had it in the forward position. That decided it. There was no more point in trying to stop. The bridge was coming at us at speed. The deck-hand, having lowered the mast, was crouching on the foredeck to await the impact of the superstructure on the edge of the bridge. The bow passed smoothly beneath and, as the arch loomed toward the wheel-house, we instinctively ducked. Nothing happened. We emerged from the far side of the bridge and looked incredulously back. It was only then that we saw it was a drawbridge. The traffic had been stopped by the lowered gates and the bridge-keeper had just started to raise the bridge, giving us the few extra inches we needed. As we were both mercifully enclosed in our respective glass-walled offices, an exchange of civilities was prevented, though the bridge-keeper's face clearly projected the trend of his thoughts.

Throughout this struggle with the controls, the *Virginia Anne* had sailed on without any perceptible change of speed. This was sinister and I resolved to approach the next obstacle a great deal more cautiously.

No sooner was the resolution made than my freedom to put it into effect was removed. The next obstacle approached in the form of a large black bow rounding the corner beyond the bridge. Stopping was out of the question, so I decided to try squeezing by the barge that with each second grew longer. Caught in a narrow channel between the barge and the bank, avoiding action on one side led us into trouble on the other and we found ourselves on another zig-zag course, to the evident astonishment of the other skipper. We were lucky to hit nothing, straightened up our course and took time off to look at the scenery and calm our nerves.

Dutch fishing village

We were still passing through an ancient village built along the banks of the canal, at this point about a foot lower than the surrounding land. Most of the houses had a diminutive patch of grass in front, and in the middle of the patch of grass an upturned dinghy. The large windows formed an exhibition of lace curtains, behind which potted plants were massed along the windowsills. Occasionally some brightly painted shutters gave a jarring stab of colour to the mellowed brick. This was Old Holland and it was easy enough to discern the picturesque quality that would attract the cameras of the summer tourists.

We had been told that our best way was through the town of Gouda and that to reach this it was necessary to turn right at a point which we calculated to be close at hand. Every so often there was an opening on the side of the canal and from a distance these looked like turnings; on closer inspection though, they proved to be small boat-yards or basins. We had passed one of these cul-de-sacs when Charlie announced that we should have gone up it. He was adamant about this and for a long time peered at the map for confirmation. 'We are going towards Amsterdam,' he stated, and 'I tell you we should have turned off back there,' jerking his thumb in the direction of the ship's wake.

Certainly the turning seemed to be a very long time in coming and we began to wonder whether Charlie had not after all been right. We asked him to go out on deck with the megaphone and find out from one of the figures bent double in the handkerchief-size vegetable gardens. Nothing happened for a bit and we wondered what he was waiting for. 'Ask that one,' I shouted from the wheel-house, as an ancient back painfully straightened itself and its owner shuffled his clogs across the fine black tilth. After a further pause there was a sound of gargling; the megaphone was still aimed haphazardly at the bank although the good man whom we had indicated was by now far behind. At length a man appeared right by the water's edge whom Charlie actually saw. All was well; we were on the right canal and the turning was very near.

We came upon it almost immediately and it was extremely sharp. Offering the usual prayer that nothing might be coming in the opposite direction, I turned the wheel and we went round as though on rails. Here was a difficult manoeuvre completed with success, but I was cheated of the momentary elation I might have felt by the sight of a swing-bridge ahead. As luck would have it, it was open and the light was green. But no; we were hardly more than two hundred yards away when the green light changed to a flashing red. I was prepared to ignore this, but as we advanced a man appeared on the central pier-pivot of the bridge and signalled to us to halt. Previous experience had taught me the futility of attempting such action in so short a distance, so by way of compromise I closed the throttle and we glided on toward the opening. I only hoped the flashing red light did not mean that the bridge was about to be closed, for it was a railway bridge and much too low to pass beneath. The man on the pier, waving at us to stop with one hand, proceeded with the other—for reasons best known to himself—to lower a long stick on which was hooked a clog. We were still moving at normal speed as we nosed between the piers of the bridge, wondering at the curious ritual being enacted before us. The clog was left hanging over the void while its owner shouted and gesticulated like a madman. The clog withdrew smartly as the wheel-house passed through the vacant space.

We asked Charlie to step outside and listen to the message, but by the time he had found his black homburg hat without which he never made a move, we were clear of the bridge and the only words he caught were 'toll bridge' and something about 'not getting away with it'. We learned later that we were supposed to put a coin, the equivalent of

2½p, into the clog. This toll was the only one we met in the whole of Holland. No other lock, bridge or quay made any charge whatsoever for the services of which we availed ourselves. When later we were in Belgium we were charged 3p at one lock, and this again was the only charge for crossing the entire country, despite the enormous cost of maintaining canals.

We were now sailing along the Gouwe Canal and likely to encounter vessels of up to 1,350 tons—sizeable craft by any standards.

Up to this point the canal had been largely sheltered by the houses lining its banks. But here we entered open country and for the first time we were subjected to the full force of the wind, a new and unnecessary hazard, blowing toward the beam. We began to be driven into the left bank and had to re-establish our course with another series of curves. The only drawback to this slanted progression was that it used a larger width of canal and if we were to pass other traffic we had first to straighten up and then to try to recover the position afterwards. On one occasion we met three barges, one behind the other, and in passing them we were blown dangerously towards the centre, helpless to correct course.

It was cold, wet and windy, yet it was strangely satisfying to sit in the shelter of the wheel-house and move steadily along at about 6 miles an hour. Although little more than the speed of a fast walk, it was amazing how swiftly the scenery changed. From the height of the wheel-house there was a breathtaking view across the landscape. It is strange how much more one can see from a barge than from a car. So many roads are penned in by walls or hedges or continuous development of some kind that the view from a car is often limited to only a few yards. Here there was a feeling of immense freedom, and even if the landscape was sometimes unattractive, it never lacked interest.

Holland is the country of great skies and limitless horizons. The clouds, drunk on the endless space, devise an ever-changing map of oceans, continents and mountains— all the drama and diversity lacking in the landscape. The familiar motifs of the Delft tile may still be seen everywhere: a man fishing from a boat beside an old bridge, a cluster of trees round a church or the inevitable windmill: these and others too still make up the incidental charm of this flat land and provide a happy shock of recognition. Only the milkmaid in her huge bonnet has passed with that leisurely age. A single tree standing out against the background of the darkening sky, a ridged meadow with cattle reflected in the water of a shallow ditch, a few reeds at the water's edge and the sloping tiled roof of an old farmhouse: these are the classic compositions of Holland. But they depend for survival on space, the thing most seriously undermined by the spread of industry and by the effects of the worst population problem in Europe.

The rain blotted out the distant horizon, serrated by the outline of development, and encouraged concentration on the attractive detail so near at hand. The canal was long and straight, the traffic sparse and for the first time I began to feel that all was under control. I was by now able to steer a reasonably straight course, even in a strongish wind, and so long as I could go on for ever without stopping I could not see that I need have a worry in the world. The engine had settled down to a steady beat and for the first time I felt that I could relax. However, we knew that just before the town of Gouda there was a lock and that the matter of stopping would have to be considered in earnest.

Locks are sacred on the waterways because to damage a gate is to put an entire canal out of commission. Repairs may take days or even weeks and during this time a vital artery of commerce is closed. I had already decided, should we be unable to stop at an unexpected lock, to steer straight for the bank and abide by the consequences. Fortunately this particular lock was plainly visible from a distance of at least half a mile and as soon as it came into sight I throttled back. As no speed seemed to be lost I went into neutral and finally into astern. After about a quarter of a mile we had lost a noticeable amount of speed but were still going at a good three or four miles an hour. I opened the throttle full; there were the usual noises and the same lack of effect. About 200 yards away our speed was down to one or two miles an hour. It was going to be a close-run thing and I found myself searching the bank for a suitable spot to ram.

There was no other traffic in sight, so it was possible to zig-zag along and gain an additional braking effect. This, combined with the feeble activity of the propeller, just sufficed to bring us to a halt 50 yards or so before the lock, alongside some mooring posts. The crew lined the deck on the port side, each with rope in hand, while we drifted imperceptibly towards the posts. We were sheltered almost entirely from the wind by tall buildings on the bank but the little there was moved the barge, without any assistance, in exactly the right direction. We were going to make a perfect mooring and the first post was coming neatly within reach of Charlie on the foredeck. When the post was beside him, he placed the noose of his rope firmly over it. We moved closer to see the exact manner in which a rope should be fastened to a ship's bollards; at last we could look forward to a practical demonstration by an expert. Charlie placed the rope round a bollard and, as the barge drifted on, payed it out, hand over hand. The distance between the ship's bollard and the mooring post increased steadily and we wondered over the subtlety of paying out so much rope. As the end of the rope came in sight, we sharpened our powers of observation so that we should not miss the sleight of hand about to be performed. Three feet, two feet, one foot and, unbelievably, Charlie *dropped* the end over the edge into the water. We stared at him incredulously. 'Rope too short,' he grunted accusingly and stood looking gloomily at the slowly sinking line.

We made fast to the next mooring post with a successful knot and turned our attention to the recovery of the rope. Its looped end was still hanging over the first mooring post at a distance of several yards from the bank. We calculated that our inexperience would be less open to detection if we recovered it by dinghy rather than by trying to manoeuvre the ship astern.

Accordingly we set about lowering the dinghy in as nonchalant a manner as possible. It was lying on the roof of the superstructure and the four of us took up positions round it. It weighs about 300 pounds and, although the weight alone is not too formidable a burden for four men, its awkward shape and lack of handholds make it a distinctly uncomfortable load. None the less we were anxious to preserve an air of familiarity with the operation and our faces wore a mask of calm assurance as the dinghy was lifted into the air. We lost a little of our confidence, it is true, as we envisaged the strain of lowering this awkward weight to the water some eight feet below the level of our feet. For if we let the dinghy straight down, bow first, it would simply fill with water and sink.

It was decided to try to lower it first to the deck and thence to the water. The party staggered toward the wheelhouse, but it became apparent that there would not be room to lower it and in a crescendo of groans the dinghy was transferred toward the bow. It was then that Charlie caught his foot on some protuberance and momentarily released his hold on the dinghy. Surprisingly it made no difference whatsoever to the balance of our load and we noted that despite the grunts and groans that Charlie had been foremost in emitting, he had not actually done more than place his hand on the edge of the boat. Incredibly, Charlie was not embarrassed by this small revelation but merely replaced his homburg more firmly on his head and stood to one side whilst the rest of us shuffled drunkenly toward the front of the ship.

I judged it was time Charlie contributed to the solving of our difficulties, since they were entirely of his own manufacture. We put the dinghy down and I took Charlie with me to the deck, the plan being for the other two to lower the dinghy to us before descending to help with the final launching. The two on top started to pass the dinghy down; the weight transferred to us rapidly and I called to Charlie to hold on until the others came to our assistance. But he abandoned a feeble effort and I could not maintain my grip. The dinghy crashed down on the edge of the barge and fell sideways into the water. The deck-hand leapt into it with great presence of mind whilst it was still within reach and we were able to hand him an oar before he too drifted away.

This unscheduled launching of the dinghy and the attendant noise and commotion had attracted the attention of everyone at the lock and our desperate efforts to hoist the dinghy on board again after the recovery of the rope were observed with unconcealed mirth.

By the time we were ready to start again, the lock had already been open for half an hour and the lock-keeper was shouting to us that he was about to close for the night. The entrance to the lock was in the form of a steady taper composed of posts set very close together and our entry was thus greatly facilitated. We were literally funnelled into the lock without having to make any complicated manoeuvres and I could concentrate all my efforts on stopping before we hit the far end. I advanced with a slowness that the lock-keeper found excruciating; doubtless he thought it deliberately contrived to make him late as retribution for having amused himself at our expense. Charlie was unwilling to explain the mechanical limitations of our vessel and my own efforts to mime a cavitating propeller were obviously considered an additional form of rudeness.

The most intriguing thing about passing through was that it was impossible to tell whether we had moved up or down as a result; the water level looked exactly the same on both sides though, as we soon discovered, this experience was by no means unique in Holland.

We emerged from the lock into a round basin some 200 yards in diameter and, as it was getting dark, planned to stay the night there. By moving from the lock at funereal speed and helped by the wind, we arrived without skill alongside a quay studded with bollards. Under cover of the growing darkness we secured ourselves with an assortment of knots which we planned to undo at first light.

The flag was lowered and removed for the night in accordance with the instructions in the Almanack, a gang plank was laid between ship and shore and a lamp run up the mast. The lamp was a compromise between remaining unlit and disposing light around the boat in compliance with regulations as yet unknown to us. Charlie offered his services over the lights, some of which were coloured, but we had had enough of his advice for one day and preferred to remain in semi-obscurity rather than have the barge dressed like a Christmas tree.

We retired below to the warmth of the interior and set about sharpening our appetites with a little Dutch gin. In this we were over-successful and soon had to admit that only a highly-skilled restaurateur could hope to remove the edge, now razor-sharp. By way of justification for a possible extravagance, we thought it appropriate to celebrate completion of our first day's travels covering some twelve miles which, although not without incident, at least had not resulted in any permanent disaster. After giving a final polish to our appetites and unsuccessfully negotiating with Charlie for the return of my overcoat we set out into the dark, lured on by the excitement of a menu studded with regional specialities and pondered over with due deliberation in the *gemütlichkeit* environment of a Dutch restaurant.

It was bitterly cold outside and the streets of Gouda were deserted. It was some time before Charlie was able to find out the wrong way to the town centre and by the time we were near, our chief concern was more for bodily warmth than for sustenance. If there were any restaurants, they were closed or camouflaged. It was as though a curfew had descended on the town; a few hurrying figures appeared briefly from time to time, disappearing without trace before they could be questioned. Perhaps our ad hoc clothing had something to do with it. Eventually we arrived in the main square and scurried round its perimeter like rats in a kitchen looking for access to food and warmth.

We were encouraged by the sight of two people coming out of what looked like a restaurant; but long before we arrived at its steamed-up windows, the nauseous smell of burnt oil and fish had blunted the remnants of our appetites and, greatly downcast, we started retracing our steps. The wind was much colder now and its force was peculiarly unaltered by the direction of the streets, making it inescapable: this too seems a characteristic of Dutch cities. With bowed heads we walked briskly past Gouda's tourist showpiece, the Gothic town hall which, together with the surrounding stalls piled high with that waxy red-coated spherical cheese to which the town has given its name (or is it the other way round?), baits the summer tourist each market-day. What a pity that one's first thought at the mention of Gouda is for this most insipid of cheeses and not for the exquisite stained glass for which the town is also traditionally famous!

The way back seemed infinitely longer and the depression we felt was only relieved by yet another Dutch peculiarity—the curious habit of not drawing the living-room curtains at night. Although this is not a universal practice, there are sufficient curtainless windows to make any nocturnal wanderer a good deal wiser about the habits of his mid-twentieth century brethren. Without exception, every family we saw was watching television, all but two of them the same programme. The window-sills were all covered with an assortment of potted plants and the only ready method of distinguishing the Joneses from the Smiths was by the colour and size of the glass ornaments which were so precisely disposed about the rooms. In spite of the greatly changed furnishings one cannot help being reminded of the interiors of, for example, Teniers. The woman of the house still sits in a state of orderly repose with her hands folded on her lap, her hair as often as not in a bun, amidst highly polished furniture; only now the television screen has replaced the spinning wheel.

By the time we reached the boat, we were frozen and we waited whilst the appropriate key was selected from a large bunch by the faint light of a far-off street lamp. But the key would not turn the lock. Others were tried. None fitted. Then the key which we knew to be the right one was tried by all in turn, still without success. Then the wrong keys were tried again until one jammed in the lock. Frozen, hungry and disillusioned, we circled the deck in the forlorn hope that a window might be open. Finally an entry was forced and, heavy with gloom and sleep, we sat disconsolate around the saloon in silent exhaustion. An attempt was made to finish the Dutch gin but its effect was greatly diminished. A sad effort to substitute bread and cheese for the dinner we had missed ended in a few feeble nibbles at a loaf that had somehow already contrived to become stale. Tired and despondent, we went to bed.

6

Suffering from wind

Our intention to leave soon after dawn came to nothing. At breakfast it was solemnly agreed that major expenditure in energy must be compensated by an equivalent food intake; something must be done to improve the catering. After breakfast I landed the mini-cycle and set off on a foraging expedition. Not a very experienced bicyclist, I found myself in difficulties among the swarms of Dutchmen on their larger and more antiquated mounts, not unlike those I was experiencing on the canals. Within quite a short distance I had caused one highly skilled cyclist to dismount and another to swerve so drastically that he was only just missed by a car. As the load on the back of the mini-cycle increased with each purchase, so too did the tendency toward unpredictable wobbling. The proprietor of a bicycle shop stared at my machine with scorn. I had just made up my mind to demonstrate for the benefit of the export trade that, though small, it was capable of a good turn of speed, when a van shot in front of me and nearly ended my days.

Safely aboard again and with a happy feeling that whatever dangers lay ahead they were as nothing to the perils of competing on a bicycle in a Dutch street, we prepared to move off.

At the far side of the basin, a swing-bridge guarded the entrance to the canal. We knew that it was customary to give warning of one's approach to bridges and locks by means of a single prolonged blast on a hooter. Accordingly, as soon as the engine had been started I leant from the wheel-house and blew the Dutch horn. The loud, sonorous note was snatched away by the wind which still blew at gale force. But I saw the gates being lowered across the road, the traffic come to a standstill and the bridge start to swing upwards. With full engine and rudder I attempted to swing the bow out to face the bridge. It moved out a short way and stopped obstinately, brought to a halt by the force of the wind. The crew answered my call for help by pushing with the boathooks. The effort required to move a 115 ton barge with a boathook is considerable, but it was just beginning to show signs of success when to my dismay I saw the bridge being lowered again. The attempt was abandoned. While I was wondering what to do next, the bridge-keeper came out of his control tower, down the steps and towards us, glad of an excuse to examine an unusual craft at close quarters. Apologising for not being able to hold up the traffic longer owing to the importance of the road, he asked whether he could be of assistance and appeared most helpfully disposed towards us. Learning of our intended route, he convinced us that it was the worst possible way. He was invited below for a cup of coffee and the map was spread out over the table. We were horrified by the passage he now proposed: although free from locks, it lay along the great tidal estuaries of the Rhine, formidable not only for their huge width and treacherous currents but for the volume of traffic, including ocean-going vessels of enormous tonnage. But he knew his subject and was firm. Finally

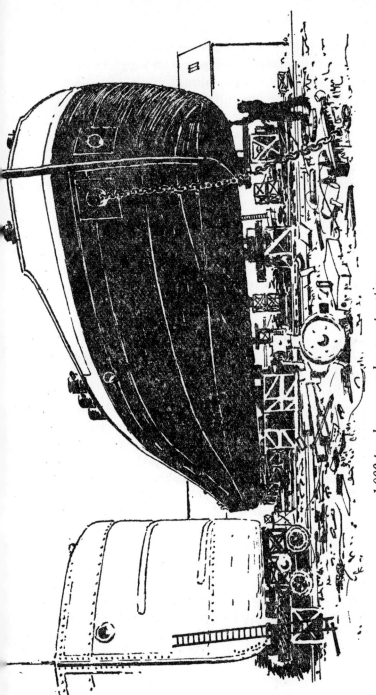

1,000-ton barges under construction

we were persuaded to compete with the giants and alter our course from east to west, sailing toward Rotterdam.

On previous visits to Holland I had seen the Rhine and I could all too clearly recall marvelling at its vast expanse one misty winter's day; it was not difficult to believe that this is indeed the busiest waterway in the world. Helped by the Meuse and by a vast interconnecting network of river, canal and estuary, it swells the Netherlands' great wealth of waterways. It ensures Holland's vital position as transhipment point for goods on their way to north-east Europe. Boats of all sizes had criss-crossed the Rhine as I watched, avoiding or making use of the current as it suited them. No longer a mere spectator now, I was full of misgivings and wondered whether the additional hazards of tide and mud-banks might not prove our undoing. It would not be long before we found out, I reflected: one mile more of canal, a lock and then the Hollandsch Ijssel, a tidal tributary of the Rhine, capable of passing 2,000 ton vessels.

The bridge-keeper returned to his post in a most co-operative spirit and, taking advantage of a temporary lull in the wind, we began the highly uncertain manoeuvre of lining up the barge with the entrance to the bridge. We fared better than before and managed to position ourselves correctly. This time the bridge-keeper had taken the precaution of opening the bridge only when we looked certain to pass, but now we saw the gates descending and the heavy flow of traffic come to a halt. The bridge-keeper was beckoning us forward with a friendly wave, keen to see us quickly through. We were aligned and poised to go. I opened the throttle cautiously. At that precise moment a sudden squall snatched at us with about as much respect as it would have shown to a paper boat and threw us against the bridge abutments. By the time we came to a halt the bow had scraped its way along until it was immediately

below the edge of the bridge. At once the stern started to
drift round and within seconds we were jammed squarely
across the entrance. The bridge-keeper, one panic-stricken
eye on the fast growing line of traffic, emerged from his
tower. Waving his arms, he started shouting instructions to
Charlie who was standing on top of the superstructure
flailing his right arm, a movement he had kept up continuously for some five minutes and which our halt had done
nothing to arrest. Charlie was far too absorbed by the importance of his own instruction to the helmsman to listen
to the bridge-keeper. During the next twenty minutes, a
dense mass of cyclists filtered to the front of the waiting
queue and the foremost were becoming visibly and audibly
impatient. The bridge-keeper was beside himself with
anxiety; had some similar incident in the past resulted in
some enraged cyclists ducking him in the canal, or was he
perhaps held personally responsible by his superiors for this
type of mishap? Whatever the reason, his distress was extreme and expressed itself in a paroxysm of operatic gesture.
From time to time a snatch of the accompanying vocal re-
frain would be carried on the wind through the wheel-
house window. Both my father and the deck-hand were now
standing on the bow, the one flailing with his left arm and
the other with his right. Any further verbal instructions
were drowned by the hooting of motor horns.

During this period of agitation I had tried moving all
the controls in all directions but, in true nightmare form,
nothing had answered. I had wondered about withdrawing
from this position and trying again. However there was
something to be said for trying to pass while the bridge was
open as it was questionable whether the bridge-keeper,
supposing he survived the ordeal, would ever again open
for us. As I hesitated, the engine in neutral, I was surprised to see the stern of the boat move away from the bank
and line itself up once more for the bridge. Without wait-

ing for another gust to blow us back, I put on full throttle and we sailed straight through, gathering speed as we went. I waved to the queue and saluted the bridge-keeper; he was leaning against the door of his office in a state of total exhaustion.

The impetus of our newly-found speed hurled us round the approaching corner. Our elation was fugitive. Stretched across the canal about a foot above the water was a steel cable; a small passenger ferry was starting out from the bank, drawing itself over to the far side by means of this cable. Certain that we could not stop in time, I blew five short blasts of the horn to indicate my loss of control. The ferry continued its crossing unperturbed. We were heading into the wind and this helped slow us down. Charlie and our deck-hand were each holding a line, hoping for something to come within range to which we could moor.

Just ahead a man was standing on a small raft, painting the side of his barge. Balanced on the outer edge of the raft was a large tin of paint and it was this that now mobilised Charlie's defective vision. A perfectly-placed bollard! As the paint tin appeared beneath him, he attempted to catch it in the noose of his line. Fortunately he missed. The owner of the paint-tin was left to ponder which we were, pirates or lunatics and, taking quick hold of the tin, clambered up a ladder into his barge. Whilst my attention had been taken up with this incident, the cable had been lowered and we passed safely by.

A short way ahead lay the last lock before the open river and as the gates opened, we slid gently in. There was only about a foot clear on each side, but largely by luck we avoided touching as we entered. I suppose I must have been expecting congratulations from the lock-keeper on this smooth entry. It therefore came all the more as a surprise when the comically foreshortened figures of two uniformed lock officials loomed up in the sky at the edge of the lock wall above us, one of them shouting authoritatively.

'They want money,' Charlie translated.

'What for?'

'The toll bridge you missed. They are very annoyed.'

I handed over the amount of the toll, slightly less than the cost of the telephone call that must have informed these worthies of our criminal intentions.

This lock raised us about six feet to the level of the river on the far side and as the gates opened we saw before us an expanse of mud exposed by the low tide. Immediately outside the lock gates we had to turn sharp right. I turned the wheel as fast as I could, but not fast enough and there can have been only a few inches of water beneath the propeller as we drifted across to the far side. I was as keen to avoid being stuck on a mud-bank as I was to avoid shipwreck itself and thereafter steered a very central course, giving the corners a wide berth.

Here the country was as depressing as Dutch country can be; indeed it is difficult to imagine anything so utterly dreary. The stark developments of mankind are the only relieving features of this grass-covered mudland separating the many mouths of the Rhine. In the eyes of Dutchmen this land has one supreme advantage: it is actually above sea level. Just what this means was brought home to me when one Dutchman was telling me about the misfortunes of another. 'He has had all this family trouble,' he concluded, then in a lowered voice 'and his house is below sea level.' We were standing outside the afflicted man's house. 'And where do you live?' I asked. 'Oh, up there,' and he jerked his hand upward as might an alpine peasant indicating his eyrie from the valley floor. The ground was barely slanted and the house which my informant owned could not have stood more than four feet above the other.

7

Small fish in a big river

The wind was now dead ahead and it cut our speed by nearly half. We had so far seen no other traffic all day and we wondered whether this might not mean that the gale was considered to be too strong. The thought was beginning to have a depressing effect on morale when a sudden playful gust of wind caught the dinghy and blew it right across the superstructure, where it lodged against a projection in a state of indecision for agonising seconds until it was secured. We were anxious not to secure it too well since it doubled as our lifeboat; on the other hand if it did blow away it was going to be of little use in that capacity.

We were sufficiently worried by the weather to speculate openly about our fate should the engine stop, and indeed its recently altered pitch should have served as a warning. Our one hope would be to anchor. Up to this moment we had paid little attention to this piece of equipment and I went to inspect it in detail. The appearance of the anchor winch was complicated by a number of wheels, a clutch and a brake. The mud anchor was lying on the deck and we fixed the end of the anchor chain to it. Although it looked solid enough, I thought I might just be able to drag it singlehanded to the edge of the boat and drop it over. I remembered stories of men who, having managed to heave the anchor over the side, noticed too late the loop of chain encircling their feet; before having time to jump clear, the chain had tightened and carried them to the bottom. With this in mind I stood well clear and tried to drag the anchor. Without success. The deck-hand came to help and together we tugged at it. Failing to make any impression at all, we fastened a rope around it and three of us pulled for all we were worth. We succeeded in moving it to the side ready to push overboard beneath the rail. But, the shaft of the anchor once over the edge, the claw part caught in a projection on the gunwale and refused to budge. The effort served only to anchor the boat to itself.

Back in the wheel-house, I noticed that the blue smoke that always came from the engine-room hatch had become far denser. Peering down inside, I could only just make out the outline of the engine. I took a deep breath and, armed with fears of fire and explosion, descended the ladder. The heroic nature of my mission unfortunately went unobserved. There was cause for alarm. It does not take a mechanic to diagnose a serious engine condition any more than it does a doctor to recognise illness.

The iron hull was reverberating to the dissonant hammerings from within the engine itself. Every few seconds the sound would shift to a new key and the engine had lost its customary sense of rhythm. Smoke was erupting from an assortment of apertures and notably from the oil-filler pipe; from this unofficial exit burst a column of oily smoke in rapid pulsations. Water was pouring freely from the bearing of the pump and the level of water in the bilges had risen alarmingly.

There is something eerie about a ship's engine-room.

There is more to it than visions of disasters caused by escaping steam or leaks. Certainly there is a background awareness of potential danger, but there is also the realisation of being below water level to increase the feeling of uneasiness. Awe in the presence of great power contributes also and if in the case of the *Virginia Anne* this power was sadly diminished, it was more than offset by the extraordinary variety and originality of the sounds produced. Be this as it may, whenever I have to be in the engine-room while on the move, I always keep one eye on the ladder to freedom. This time my discomfort was increased when I saw the frequent, sudden turnings of the steering gear and the repeated attempts to open the throttle still further. Confident that I was prey to some hideous danger, I emerged from the engine-room hatch with what I considered to be exactly that combination of urgency and restraint that becomes a ship's captain.

The sickness of the engine and the increasing violence of the wind had between them reduced speed to the point where we were not progressing at all. We were becoming a helpless victim to the elements and should have to moor as soon as possible and send the chief engineer about his business. But where and to what were we to tie up? A gently sloping mud-bank lined both sides of the river and for some time there had been no sign of a quay.

Attempts were made to relieve the tension with a rather forced wit. But not so Charlie who, silent for the past hour, now openly speculated on our fate.

'Shouldn't have come this way,' he suggested helpfully. Then, after a pause:

'Don't expect the anchor will hold in this wind.' Another pause, and

'Ought to have gone the other way; told you so!'

A momentary slackening of the wind allowed us to inch our way round the next bend with agonising slowness. A

81

F

jetty projected into the river on the right. Our spirits rose until we were near enough to see that the end of the jetty was only some twelve feet across. It was going to be difficult to end up with the centre of the boat opposite the mooring posts. If we secured only the bow or the stern, the boat would be blown round—the jetty acting as pivot—and we should conclude the manoeuvre on the mud on one or other side.

As we came out of the bend, the wind started to blow abeam the barge. Seconds later the bow struck the furthest post of the jetty and forced it far out to one side. We swung round and struck the other three posts simultaneously; all were loosened but remained more or less upright. Out of any semblance of control, we carried on past the jetty, ran briefly aground on what sounded like sharpened stones, swung round as effortlessly as a compass needle and found ourselves facing the opposite direction. Still helpless, we repassed the jetty, knocking the other corner post askew, drifted in toward the bank, struck something solid with the bow, swung round again in the wind and once again approached the jetty. Miraculously the propeller had not fouled the bottom. Clearly it was now or never and with a frantic wheel-spinning and a gear-changing that must have simulated the action of a demented cook stirring some monstrous Christmas pudding, we arrived, with frightening precision and entirely by chance, square alongside the middle of the jetty. Charlie, as we had come to expect of him, threw his line into the water, but my father and the deck-hand managed to weave a spider's web of rope around the remaining posts. The entire jetty was wobbling like a jelly.

Our mooring achieved, my worries of the past hour shifted focus as I awaited the emergence from the house at the far end of the jetty of an irate figure who no doubt at this moment was telephoning for his solicitor and an escort of river police. But minutes passed and no door opened. I descended into the bilges to see whether by any foul chance our groundings had caused a leak. All was fortunately well and I returned to the engine-room to offer my services in the dismantling of the engine. My arrival however coincided with the ejection of Charlie who in the space of two or three minutes had almost succeeded in losing an indispensible nut, threatening the engine's survival. He had also, as I now noticed, managed to spill oil down my overcoat. Profiting by Charlie's experience, I admitted to myself that engines were best left in the hands of those who knew their mysteries and turned my attention to the making of coffee.

Our immediate mechanical difficulties apparently derived from no more sinister cause than the oiling up of several plugs and it was not long before we were ready to start again. We cast off and proceeded with altogether renewed vigour toward Rotterdam.

The river gradually widened as corner succeeded corner until an hour or so later we reached the junction of the Ijssel and the Lek (or Lower Rhine), just east of Rotterdam. The Ijssel had widened into an extremely large river, one side of which was entirely given over to shipbuilding. As the junction came in sight, we were appalled by the amount of traffic. Emerging from the deserted Ijssel, we now had to cross this torrent of shipping in order to turn back up the Lek, the northernmost of the two 2,000 ton waterways of the Rhine estuary. We continued on our way hoping for a break in the flow, but there were never less than a dozen assorted ships in passage at any one moment. The size of some of these seemed unbelievable to a landsman. Most were sea-going tankers of several thousand tons, but there were numerous cargo ships and any number of barges too, all substantially larger than ours. We never saw a vessel smaller than our own, except for the tugs, all the time we were on the estuaries of the Rhine. And yet we ourselves felt incredibly bulky when it came to carrying out some delicate manoeuvre.

Already past the junction with no suspicion of a break in the stream of traffic, it was obvious that we should have to turn regardless if we were not to be swept on to Rotterdam. It was difficult to know quite how to announce our intention. It seemed unlikely that the plaintive sound of the mouth-blown horn would find its way to those elevated bridges and we were in any case unsure of the number of blasts that indicated a 'U' turn. Was one supposed to flash a light or stand on the roof and make a hand signal? In the end we settled for two methods. Charlie was despatched to stand on the roof and hold out his left arm while our deckhand blew an assortment of long, medium and short blasts on the horn. Whenever he blew too hard the note went up an octave and there was a moment when I thought I detected a bar from Mozart's Third Horn Concerto. We pulled over to the centre of the river and began the turn. About a third of the way round, our intention suddenly became clear to a heavily-laden barge of forbidding size that had appeared from nowhere and was now bearing down toward a position that we intended as our own in about ten seconds' time. The skipper blew an outraged blast on his very large horn and altered course by not so much as one degree. I turned as fast as I could to achieve a parallel course and seconds later he passed us, inches away, at great speed. I looked the other way.

My confidence shaken by this frustrating attempt to turn, it was some minutes before I felt like trying again. When I did, however, I thought I had chosen an especially favourable moment to make the manoeuvre unmolested, with

A small fish in a big river

only one small cargo ship coming up from behind and nothing at all immediately ahead. I estimated that if I hurried, the ship behind would still not be opposite me until I had completed the turn. As it happened it passed our stern in mid-turn with very little room to spare. The skipper expressed himself freely.

For an hour we moved up the Lek (or lower Rhine as it really is), then turned into the cross-channel known as the Noord waterway (one of the interconnections between Rhine and Meuse, limited to 500 ton boats) and two hours later came through part of the old Meuse or Merwede to Dordrecht. All the way we passed shipping of enormous variety and size, again up to 2,000 tons. Any number of shipyards echoed to the sound of hammering and blazed with pinpoints of incandescent light from the welders. We passed a ship-breaker's yard where mountains of dismantled equipment lay rusting to a uniform colour. There was something very sad about the ships awaiting their turn to be broken up as they lay at anchor along the river, like cattle lined up at a slaughter-house; a life about to be ended, the end met with resignation and dignity. Occasionally the rotting hull of an ancient wooden barge would project from the mud at the river's edge, its exposed ribs black with age, an unburied carcass.

Dordrecht claims the distinction of being the oldest town in the province of South Holland. As in so many river- and canal-side towns. the oldest part lies along the waterfront and we could study it at leisure from our unique vantage point. Its position today as a major shipbuilding centre has imposed on the old town that we saw much that is modern, but both elements co-exist peaceably.

As we embarked gingerly upon our course up the Waal, another exit for the waters of the Rhine, we had the benefit of the wind behind us and despite the width of the river —over half a mile—it was encouraging to see the speed with which the various landmarks sped past. It was not until I left the wheel-house that I realised that we were in fact being chased up the river by a rising tide and a following gale of great intensity. The wheel-house door could only be shut with difficulty and the wind was whipping the waves into a whitening mass. The *Virginia Anne* was pitching slightly but rolling hardly at all, and her behaviour in these obviously testing conditions gave us a sense of some security.

It occurred to us to inspect the level of petrol in the tank. We were only just in time, for it was almost empty. Leaving aside for the moment the appalling calculation of petrol consumption in terms of miles per gallon, or vice versa, we had to procure more, and quickly. We were keeping as near as we dared to the south bank of the river so as to avoid the roughest water and the heaviest shipping which shared the centre. Seeing a small tanker coming up behind us, we asked Charlie to find out where was the nearest refuelling point. Someone emerged just then from the tanker's interior to jettison a bucket of rubbish and we aimed Charlie on the appropriate bearing. 'Shout now!' we instructed, but nothing happened. 'Quick!' we urged and still the megaphone was silent, for Charlie could not yet see his quarry. He was realigned and this time emitted his distinctive gargling sound. The good man was not to be deterred so easily from his task of emptying his rubbish and preferred to pick out the contents piece by piece, perhaps with a nostalgia for the succulent meals of which each reminded him. He said nothing but finally pointed to the north shore then eclipsed by his own boat. His ship's name was written in the Cyrillic alphabet and this probably accounted for his reticence for, although no flag was being worn, this dour man was no doubt from eastern Europe. We wondered whither he was bound.

Binoculars revealed the trade mark of a well-known

petrol company. We turned at once and ran the gauntlet of the other ships. On approaching, we saw that this petrol station was in fact a large converted barge secured about 100 yards from the shore by piles driven into the river bed. To reduce the risk of sparks, its iron side was covered in as many old motor tyres as it was possible to fit. While the refuelling operation was in progress, I disembarked and found that the interior was fitted up as a ship's chandlery. Various purchases were made. We asked after the best place to spend the night and learned that it would be very unwise to go further than absolutely necessary, that the weather was still deteriorating, snow being forecast, and that even motorists were being warned of the danger of having their vehicles blown over in exposed areas. Thus encouraged, we lost no time in setting off once more and securing the protection of a harbour. As I left the chandlery, my spirits were low and I was bitten by a dog. Worse was to come.

Our chance of success at going it alone being rated low, we were pulled out by tug from the filling station and given a helpful push in the right direction. Our destination was the 'Emergency Harbour' at Gorinchem, about one hour's sailing. The light was already beginning to fade when Gorinchem came in sight and the harbour to which we had been sent proved to be nothing more than a narrow creek flanked on one side by mooring posts and on the other by mud and reeds. We had thought naïvely that it owed its name to its suitability for ships in an emergency, but now saw that the nature of the harbour itself constituted the emergency. We were not long in having our suspicions confirmed as the wind took command of us and drove us defenceless into the mud and reeds. As we swept broadside into the rushes, we flushed a flight of duck. I suspected that this time we should have to concede defeat.

Providentially—as we thought at the time—but by design as we afterward suspected, a tug appeared and threw us a line. We were taken in tow into the main harbour and relieved of a generous sum of money.

The quay to which we had been taken could not be seen for a line of large barges. To these a second and third line were made fast. We formed part of a fourth row and in order to land had to climb over the three others. Soon after we arrived, still more barges pulled in and the harbour was soon filled with a fifth, sixth and seventh row. We felt very insignificant sandwiched between so many other larger boats, some of them up to 1,500 tons.

We made the acquaintance of our neighbours and heard news that chilled the blood. The entire fleet surrounding us would be moving out soon after five o'clock the following morning, while it was still dark. We had the alternative of trying to stay where we were by manoeuvring our way to the quay through the swarm of departing barges, or going with them. In either event it would be pitch dark. We opted for the latter course as being the simpler and asked our neighbour whether we might follow him out of the harbour. He readily agreed and offered to hammer the roof at 4.30, in case we were not awake.

Copying the others, we made ready the navigation lights, charged the batteries and went below to organise dinner.

Outside it was freezing hard, but inside the temperature was 75°. What a wonderful sensation it was, and one that never palled, to come down to this heat and relax with a glass of Dutch gin after having become so thoroughly chilled on deck! One could feel the cold being driven out by a sense of well-being stronger than I have ever felt on land. In this atmosphere the tinned meal we had prepared again became a feast. Charlie, who never lacked a sense of occasion, chose the moment that we had assembled at table to shave. Plucking an electric razor from his pocket, he sat down at his place and started the apparatus. Fortunately this revolting habit was not again repeated. My appetite gone, I swallowed my share and collapsed on my bed as soon as I could.

8

Canal by compass

My sleep was punctuated with nightmares, the last of them a particularly vivid portrayal of the ship being repeatedly thrown against a rock. In reality it was our neighbour hammering the roof. I had foolishly left the window open and despite the heating it was bitter. The thought of getting up could not have been less attractive but I could hear our deck-hand on the move and there were barely twenty minutes before we were due to be pushed off.

Outside the wind blew with undiminished strength and coldness; it was a form of torture to stay on deck for more than a minute or two. Our neighbour was of course up and had already started his engine. My father, carrying out the engine-room routine of turning taps and switches, called up that all was ready. I pressed the button; the engine turned but did not start. The prospect of being cast adrift in the Rhine estuary at night, engineless, in the teeth of an icy gale, was too awful to contemplate. I tried again, but the battery showed signs of rapidly failing strength. One or two of the peripheral boats were starting to leave and our position looked ugly.

I called to the deck-hand to go and crank the engine while I pressed the starter. Mercifully the engine responded before I felt bound to exchange places with the deck-hand and through slow degrees to rotate the appallingly heavy handle.

Our neighbour was cursing the other barges for the lateness of their early start and informed us that he would be off as soon as he could see a way through. We could not make out how he was going to manage this, for we could see from the surrounding ships' lights that many more would have to sail before there would be an easy passage through. The position was little altered when about five minutes later he announced that he was leaving. We were still secured alongside him and he signalled to us to leave the ropes as they were.

I shall never know how it was done. Within minutes we had been manoeuvred through a maze of barges, occasionally serving as our neighbour's battering ram although— such was his skill—never feeling the slightest jolt. The whole operation was carried out in complete darkness since the use of headlights is forbidden; navigation lights of course throw no forward light and are there only to be seen by others. It was sometimes impossible to know whether we were going forward or backward, but I tried my best to keep in phase with my neighbour and shift the gear lever accordingly. Once or twice I found myself out of phase. It made not the slightest difference to his efforts; the huge engines in these vessels enable them to manoeuvre in a manner that was becoming a source of increasing envy to me.

After we had been taken out into the middle of the harbour, we were cast off with instructions from our benefactor to keep close behind. I concentrated on his stern light, knowing that if I once lost sight of it we should be completely lost. From the start it was obvious that we could not keep up with him, but he enabled us to clear the harbour beacons before his lamp lost itself in the ribbon of navigation lights that bewildered us as we emerged into the Rhine.

The very first signs of dawn were now visible and the impenetrable blackness of night was giving way to a uniform grey against which nothing stood out clearly. The shipping lights, shore lights and marker beacons became indistinguishable from one another in a rising mist and the flat line of the horizon merged without trace into sky and river.

As part of the ship's equipment I had brought with me a compass. Its purchase had caused some mirth amongst friends who considered that it would be about as useful to me as to a train driver, for the thin line representing the inland waterways on a map of Europe suggests that there can be little room for error in navigation.

I spread the map on the wheel-house table and, with the aid of a torch, set it to the now indispensable compass. As far as I could see we needed to aim a notch or two north of east and I steered accordingly. I will not pretend that there was any great degree of precision in our compass course, but events did prove that it prevented us making a possibly fatal error. The turning in question was much less conspicuous than we had imagined and the landmarks that had been indicated to us were scarcely visible in that deceptive light. In many places the river was overflowing its banks and only some occasional willows marked the intended bounds. Unnerved by all these difficulties, we were late in making the turn into the Afged Maas (an arm of the Meuse connecting with the Waal), a fact we could not afford to ignore when the top of a gate post suddenly materialised beside the bow. The ship started to throb, indicating dangerously little water beneath the bottom. We steered back into an area of water where nothing actually projected

above the surface and tried again to make out the course
of the river between the intermittent willows. There was a
buoy from time to time but, as it was seldom followed by
a second, it was of little use. The traffic on this reach was
light, a fact we regarded with mixed feelings, for although
we were certainly relieved to be out of the way of the larger
vessels, we could have been helped by more barges following a definite route. Having already crossed one field, we
particularly wanted to avoid running aground under these
conditions of flood and being left high and dry in a meadow
throughout the summer as a tourist attraction.

As it became lighter we noticed a slight improvement in
the scenery. The foreground, and often the middle distance
too, was no longer spoilt by uninterrupted building. The
water went to join the grassland, dispensing with the intervening stretch of mud, and a scattering of trees helped to
enliven a landscape that would otherwise have been as
dreary as it was to the north.

Just to the west of us lay the *Biesbosch*, or reed forest, an
area of about 40 square miles devastated by flood as long
ago as 1421. Seventy-two towns and villages were destroyed
and over 100,000 people drowned. We were reminded yet
again that, but for polders, much of Holland would today
be under water.

The principle of impoldering and its role in Holland's
farming industry have been set out clearly, if somewhat
over-simply, by the Czech writer, Karel Capek. 'You take a
bit of sea,' he writes, 'fence it and pump it out, and at the
bottom is left a deposit to which a very respectable slice of
Europe, by means of its rivers, supplies its best swampy soil,
and the sea its finest sand; the Dutchman drains it and sows
grass there, the cows feed on it, the Dutchman milks them
and then makes cheese, which at Gouda or Alkmaar is sold
to England. . .'

Dykes alone are sufficient for small land-reclaiming

schemes. From the primitive banks built in pre-Roman times to control the normal rise of the tide to the highly sophisticated, massive basalt or granite structures raised on ferro-concrete piles, the common purpose is to offer protection from the sea, to guide rivers and to guard the adjacent canals. Some dykes are for canalised rivers; in these cases parallel dykes are built to reinforce the banks of rivers which are then deepened and kept permanently supplied with water. One example is the New Merwede Canal from Amsterdam to the Rhine.

But reclamation schemes of any size demand the total enclosure of marshy areas by encircling dykes. The water is pumped out, leaving the reclaimed land, or polder.

The practice of impoldering on any large scale dates back only to the fourteenth century or so when windmills made heavy pumping possible for the first time. Now steam and electricity have modernised procedure.

Maybe to most people a Dutch dyke is simply a thing into which the hero of all Dutch children inserted his finger to prevent an incipient leak from developing into a catastrophic flood. But to a newly-converted, helplessly intoxicated bargee, it all added up to roughly 2,000 miles of navigable canal waiting to be explored.

9

Blue smoke and a nasty cough

After ten miles of the Afged Maas, we turned into the Maas itself (Meuse in French) and lost much of our speed to the current. A dramatic skyscape clearly augured some new ill-fortune; it was a safe enough assumption anyhow. It had become a morning of dark low cloud and there had already been some brief but icy showers. Now a single shaft of sunlight lit the water ahead of us. Looking back, I saw that the whole sky had turned to indigo. One huge cloud was striding toward us, bearing down on us, obliterating all vision behind. Now we were in the middle of the patch of sun and the grass was glowing emerald against the inky sky. All at once, as though at the touch of a switch, the sun vanished and we were in a blizzard. A squall struck the barge with such violence that we were blown to the very edge of the river before we knew what was happening. It needed a great deal of rudder to keep in the stream and in less than a minute the wheel-house windows were plastered deep with snow. Soon the whole landscape turned white, interrupted only by the black scar of the river.

G

When after some three hours we turned out of the Maas into the cut marking the start of the Zuidwillemsvaart Canal,* it was with feelings of great relief as of an ordeal safely passed. We were now entering sheltered water and competition from other barges would be limited to those of 600 tons or less. The exposed tidal estuaries with their heavy shipping were behind us and we had weathered conditions that we afterward learned had daunted many a more experienced crew. We were bursting with confidence; surely by comparison anything would be plain sailing.

In front of us lay the first lock of the canal, completed in 1826, whose 54 miles and 18 locks would cut off some 40 miles of the twisting Meuse. There were no other boats waiting and it had every aspect of being an easy mooring. As though to make a mockery of our new-found confidence, we missed the mooring, the bow somehow passing between two of the posts. The stern was dragged round by the wind and left us facing the wrong way. With some ignominy we had to go back to the Maas and turn again. Our next attempt was more successful and we were soon joined by three other barges. The gates opened, the red lights turned to green and we moved confidently in. We calculated that there would be room for one other barge and congratulated ourselves on having beaten the others to the lock. To our amazement, not only a second but also a third barge was called forward. Somehow they were accommodated and we watched for the gates to close. Instead the bow of the fourth barge nosed its way into the entrance. It seemed impossible to find room for it, but it is part of the lock-keeper's job to understand the geometric possibilities of his lock. It would just fit if advantage were taken of every inch and by sheer engine power the fourth barge forced its way in and pinned us against the far wall.

See Notes

I feared for my ship lest the force crush or indent her plates, for she was much the smallest of the four. We ran anxiously round the sides trying to insert a fender here and a tyre there to take the shock, but it was a losing battle. If I was worried in a ship of 115 tons, how must the owner of a yacht with a wooden hull feel? How could it possibly survive, sandwiched between such formidable masses?

The gates behind us were closed and some ten minutes later the front gates opened. We did not seem to have risen very much and just as we were leaving we saw that in fact the gates at the other end of the lock were already open again, presumably ready to admit another group of barges to this curious ritual. No-one seemed to resent the performance and we could only think that it must be a method of maintaining full employment in the Union of Lock-keepers.

Soon we entered the ancient cathedral town of 's Hertogenbosch and after passing the lock in the centre of the town, found a good mooring within a stone's throw of a large ship's chandlery. We were unlikely to find a better place for some much-needed maintenance and planned to stay until we had seen to everything.

We could hardly believe that we had embarked on our cruise less than forty-eight hours before. We had been so preoccupied with the business of the moment that there had not been time for a second's reflection on the happenings of each hour. It seemed now as though events of three days ago were part of another era. We were glad of the chance to stay put for a short while to recover from our exhaustion.

The day we spent in 's Hertogenbosch we might have been sailors appreciating shore leave after a long spell at sea. We visited the ship's chandler to inspect his wares and to ask why the name of the town began with an apostrophe. We were told that the name meant 'of the Duke's wood'. Thus satisfied, we left the shop without making an immediate purchase, to the obvious disgust of the proprietor. I made a mental note to avoid buying anything from him during our stay, but the choice was soon to be taken out of my hands by the Fates in the usual manner.

My father busied himself with the engine and we even managed to interest Charlie in making a thorough examination of the bilge pump. This vital piece of equipment had stopped functioning properly and had to be primed with great quantities of water before it would pump at all. The secret of this operation, as we now explained in detail to Charlie, was to unscrew the priming plug, pour in a kettleful of water, at the same time pumping furiously with the other hand; then, as soon as the pump started acting, to screw back the plug as quickly as possible. Charlie followed the instructions minutely, peering myopically at the hole into which he was pouring the water and savagely working the pump with his free hand. He was totally unprepared for the jet of bilge water, oil and sludge that caught him without warning full in the face. It was a disconcerting experience. He emerged on deck trembling with rage. This burst of activity on the part of the pump proved to have been its swan song. It was dismantled and taken to a garage for repairs.

As we expected, the mechanic reappeared after a period of gestation and, scarcely bothering to camouflage his pleasure, pronounced it beyond repair. There was nothing for it but to humble myself and return to the chandler to buy a new one.

This mishap necessitated a visit to the bank. Charlie, still extremely put out by what must have been the most humiliating event of his professional career, was asked to find out the way to the nearest bank. He accepted with uncharacteristic enthusiasm and soon returned with a street-by-street description of the shortest route. My father and I set forth into a horizontal blizzard; within seconds we were stunned into silence by the piercing cold and fought our way grimly forward. The journey seemed endless and we appeared to be making a tour of the perimeter of the town. The streets were entirely deserted and after a bit I began to appreciate Joshua's feelings as he encircled Jericho for the seventh time. An unkind thought occurred to me that we were the victims of Charlie's revenge. We finally branched off toward the town centre, stopping for that incomparable tonic, hot coffee and Dutch gin. It was scarcely the day to appreciate the charms of this old town, but even under these depressing conditions the striking beauty of the late Gothic Cathedral of St John stopped us in our tracks, if but briefly.

The next day, our new pump fitted, we awoke to more snow. It continued on and off for several days in sudden violent showers so timed as to coincide with our attempts to moor. Visibility beyond the bow would suddenly fail and then anything could, and did, happen.

Our red ensign attracted great attention and some bargees seemed to take it for granted that we had crossed the North Sea. Everyone wanted to know where we were going. Paris, we told them, at that time our long-term objective, only to find eyebrows raised in surprise. For most of the traffic we met was going only as far as Maastricht, though there was the occasional Belgian barge from Liège. If the mention of Paris impressed so, I thought it might be interesting to name an even longer-term objective and subsequent enquirers were told Marseille. Their eyes nearly dropped from their sockets with amazement and I could not resist carrying this ocular experiment further with Bordeaux. But Bordeaux might have been Kamchatka for all the response I got and the few who had heard of it disbelieved me, so the experiment had to be abandoned.

We were waiting to enter a lock one day after a morning of pitifully small progress and I was negotiating the purchase of a stale loaf with an itinerant vendor when a car suddenly drew up beside me and out stepped the previous owner of the *Virginia Anne*.

Such is the bond between boat and owner that she had been unable to sleep since we left her at the start of the journey. She had been prey to nightmares about the fate of her beloved boat and the papers had been full of accounts of the shipping disasters caused by the gales. The paper that very morning had concentrated on the havoc played in the Rhine estuary and reported the loss without trace of a boat of similar tonnage to ours, belonging to a foreigner. The strain had been too much and she had followed our course until she had found us. She was signed on as cook.

The next day was Sunday when all navigation ceases in Holland. We had originally hoped to reach the Belgian border before nightfall, but darkness caught us four locks away. Several barges overtook us and pressed on through the darkness; again we wondered at their uncanny ability to steer in the pitch dark without any lights whatsoever.

The arable Brabant countryside through which we next passed was uninspiring. Although much less built on, it was as flat as could be and the insignificant lift afforded by the locks scarcely helped to give the illusion of changing contours which we presumed to be the object of their construction. The line of the canal remained square with the straight edges of the fields, each lined with its water-filled ditch and carefully-spaced poplars. Heaps of manure, identical in size, were placed in neat rows along the parallel ribs of the ridged and furrowed fields. The random configuration of the occasional herd of cows must have been a source of anguish to the orderly farmers.

Our journey along the Zuidwillemsvaart was interrupted by draw-bridges at each intersection with a road. Rather than build ramps to raise the level of the bridges by a further eight or ten feet, which would have allowed the passage of most of the boats we saw on the canal, the Dutch have installed modern draw-bridges. These call for the full-time attendance of a bridge-keeper to press the button which lowers the gate against the traffic and raises the hinged span into an almost vertical position. By this arrangement, the time of the bridge-keeper, the road user and the barge crew can all be wasted equally. The bridge-keeper seems to make a practice of not raising the bridge until an oncoming barge has gone to the trouble of stopping and mooring. The traffic in its turn is then held up for longer as the barge, instead of passing quickly, moves slowly from its moorings. No doubt this bolsters up the feeling of self-importance innate in most uniformed petty officials the world over.

We encountered more of these inflated, humourless beings at the frontier. Of course the papers were not in order. Charlie had the job of arguing with his kinsmen but seemed overawed by their officiousness. While the officials indulged themselves in an orgy of red tape, a band of very shrewd merchants were offering us the inventory of a department store 'at prices which we should not meet again in Belgium or France'. Against this assurance, I made several purchases and it was not until I found I had been charged the equivalent of one pound for a few pieces of wood with which to mend a duck-board that I saw the double meaning. Many of the purchases were then regurgitated. No-one seemed in the least offended; no doubt this frequently happened when they pushed their luck too far and, to obviate any hard feelings, we were presented with a hideous copper and pink glass candlestick, the base of which—used alone—doubled as a vase.

The Belgian officials were happily concerned more with seeing the barge than with our papers and we were soon on our way again. During our stop we had refuelled and taken the opportunity to calculate the fuel consumption since the start of the journey. Double-checking made the result no less alarming: we had averaged only a fraction over one mile to the gallon. I began to look upon the engine with an intense dislike and to plot against it with the singleness of purpose peculiar to the victim of a financial disaster.

I decided that the engine must go and, whatever the cost, a diesel be installed. But where could such a major undertaking be attempted? The nearest large town was Maastricht but that was in Holland and, having obtained a permanent exit visa at the frontier, we could not re-enter without special permission and this would all take time. Liège seemed our only hope; there was nothing for it but to continue to feed the gluttonous engine at the rate of a gallon a mile until Liège. There I would see that justice was done to this monstrous machine.

The Belgian section of the Zuidwillemsvaart passed through country that was more attractive than its Dutch counterpart although there was an air of greater poverty about the land and buildings. In fact there is perhaps no stronger aid to the natural beauty of a region than the poverty of its inhabitants; there are no new buildings to clash with the harmony of the surroundings and time has bestowed on the older ones a mellowness that is attractive in itself. We passed some large brickworks dating from the last century. They must have been hideous when new, but they no longer actively displeased.

Whereas in Holland we had had to submit to a lock about every three miles, the Belgians had dispensed with this formality and we now embarked on a stretch of some thirty miles without a single lock or movable bridge. We made good progress and the engine, recognising the extremity of its position, set a new standard of performance. By dusk we were approaching the stretch of canal which has its western bank in Belgium and its eastern bank in Holland, just north of Maastricht.

We were looking for a sheltered spot to spend the night when the engine, unable to keep up the pretence any longer, began to splutter threateningly. We steered toward the bank where we ran aground with an agonising scraping sound. Part of the bank had collapsed and we passed over the submerged heap of stones and came to rest with the stern firmly grounded. The wind caught the bow and once again swung us round to face the opposite bank. Pushing from the stern with long poles achieved nothing. We were preparing to row across in the dinghy to the other side with a rope which we would fasten to a tree in an attempt to winch ourselves off, when a barge unexpectedly rounded the corner. We flashed a lamp at it through the darkness, but the skipper made no effort to stop and somehow squeezed by between our bows and the far bank. The wash lifted us off the stones.

The following day the motor ceased functioning altogether. We happened to be passing a small, empty port at the time and with our remaining speed tried to moor. But as usual we had reckoned without the wind which took control of us, turned us right round like a weather vane and despatched us backwards along the canal. We were in a most unpleasant situation. Had it not been for the immaculately dressed bespectacled man standing on the towpath, apparently lost in meditation, we might have drifted to our downfall there and then. He started violently when a rope was flung at him, together with instructions to tie it round a bollard issued in Dutch, French and, for good measure, English. He obeyed instantly and within minutes we were safely moored.

We introduced ourselves and our rescuer generously placed himself entirely at our disposal. I explained that we needed a mechanic, a taxi and a bank. A mechanic and a taxi were procured, the taxi being required for my father who had to return to England and who had volunteered to take Charlie with him to a point from which he could be returned to Amsterdam. Poor Charlie! After he had gone I felt sorry for him. The crew was now reduced to three.

The visit to the bank was memorable. I had been advised not to accept the proffered rate of exchange without at least a discussion. It had never before occurred to me that the matter was open to negotiation and I was hesitant.

'Please may I change some travellers' cheques for Belgian francs?'

'Certainly. How many please?'

'It depends on the rate,' I suggested tentatively.

'It's the official rate,' quoting a rate of exchange.

'But it varies and the rate you give is not very attractive,' I ventured.

'It has gone down today. Yesterday was better and the day before that was better still.'

'I see. Then may I cash my cheques the day before yesterday, please?'

'I will ask the Manager. Just a moment please.'

He returned a few minutes later, all smiles.

'Yes, that is in order. The Manager says that one day is very much like another.'

By the time the mechanic arrived, the deck-hand and I were already hard at work on the engine. The engine-room was full of petrol from the stripped carburettor and our air intake was limited to only one hatchway as once again it was snowing hard. Glancing up, I saw the legs of the mechanic descending the iron ladder, followed in due course by his head. I saw to my horror that he was smoking, leapt to my feet, seized the cigarette from his mouth and threw it outside. The needle on the explosive-vapour indicator in the wheel-house was reading 'Explosive mixture—maximum danger'. The mechanic was unmoved; no doubt he was the type that smoke while welding petrol tanks and ultimately die for their bravado. He was unhelpful about the engine. His diagnosis changed every minute and we were relieved when he announced that he would go and fetch his father.

Calculating that we had just half an hour before the father could possibly return, we set to in a frantic effort to effect the repair before he arrived. The name of the nearby town was Rekem, ominously, and having seen the son at work we had no wish to be blown up by the father.

In my haste I dropped several nuts into the bilge where they disappeared deep under age-old oil, lost for ever. After making a number of alterations within, we put as much of the engine together again as we could find, opened the hatches wide, waited tense minutes for the indicator to reach a safe reading and pressed the starter. The engine started at once and, notwithstanding several unexplained oil leaks, had never gone better.

We moved off before the wreckers came into sight, turning to the right to avoid re-entering Holland. We passed through two locks, raising us a total of some forty feet to the level of the Meuse at Liège.

We now entered the Albert Canal, an immensely impressive piece of engineering.* Built on a vast scale, it connects the Scheldt estuary and Antwerp to Liège and throughout its 81 miles has only some 7 locks, giving a total rise of 60 metres overall. It is open to ships of up to 2,000 tons. Napoleon himself urged the building of this waterway, but it was not completed until 1848. We had been told that it was very busy but this, like much of the information we received, was quite inaccurate. We passed only a handful of large ships during our 20 mile run along its southern end, and even one nearly as small as ours.

Soon after joining the canal, we passed through very high cuttings which terminated in a gigantic cut over 200 feet deep. The sides of the canal were built in stone and sloped well back so that it was never possible to get within reach of the bank to moor. As the day progressed, we began to look anxiously about for a port or quay against which we could tie up for the night but, apart from one or two factory quays which were already occupied, there was no-

*See Notes

Albert Canal

where. With the growing darkness, the matter assumed a greater urgency. It was going to be a clear, cloudless night but without moonlight. The wind had dropped and it was very cold. The thermometer in the wheelhouse registered four degrees below freezing. Brief sorties were made to place the navigation lights.

Soon it was completely dark, although there were just sufficient buildings along the bank for us to be able to discern the approximate course of the canal from the reflection of their lights. We were still at least six miles from Liège and the junction with the Meuse and we had no intention of getting involved with the Meuse's swift current in the pitch dark of an icy winter's night.* Two miles further on we came to a deserted-looking quay in front of some derelict buildings. In the distance the sky was bright with the lights of Liège and against this background were silhouetted the black, jagged ruins we were now approaching. The place was as sinister as a scene in a thriller and I half expected to pick out in the beam of the searchlight a stabbed corpse lying on the quay.

During the night our mooring ropes worked loose. We had drifted several feet from the quay, although we were still attached to a bollard by one line. The first barge of the day came past at dawn and its wash sent us crashing into the wall. The noise was terrific and the impact dislodged an assortment of objects. My first impression on being startled into consciousness was that we were sinking. I felt sure another boat had struck us and made for the window, prompted by the instinct of self-preservation. I tore the curtains aside expecting to see the water lapping at the glass, but outside everything looked perfectly normal. The subsiding wash of the barge, now already passed from sight, revealed the cause of the commotion. The others had experienced a similar awakening and we decided that as we

*See Notes

were still afloat we might as well move off and make an early start.

A heavy mist obscured vision much beyond the far side of the canal, here some 200 feet wide, and we moved forward with great caution. The last lock of the Albert Canal was open and we emerged with some misgiving into the swollen waters of the Meuse. High on our left stood the colossal statue of King Albert, standing guard over the entrance to the canal bearing his name. Silhouetted against the grey mist, the face of this much-loved king conveyed most forcibly the monarch's dignity and isolation.

The effects of the swift current lost no time in making themselves felt and within the first 200 yards we had lost three quarters of our speed. The prospect of engine failure did not bear contemplation and in silent determination we awaited the horribly drawn-out arrival of Liège's many bridges. As we progressed imperceptibly toward the city centre, the river narrowed slightly and the current concentrated its force between the more constricted banks. The bridges themselves presented terrifying obstacles, for their massive piers compressed still further the course of the water and there was actually a noticeable difference in water level, a step, between one side of each bridge and the other. The river was deserted and there was no hope of throwing a line to a passing barge for a tow. The anchor would be our only hope if anything went wrong and we were not too hopeful of its prospects of finding a hold strong enough to withstand the power of this river in flood.

Liège is surrounded by hills and is situated the better part of 200 miles from the mouth of the Meuse—less than half its navigable distance—at the point where it is met by the river Ourthe, also partly navigable.* Previous inspection of the map had given no hint that this innocent-look-

See Notes

ing blue line would in reality prove to be a rapid river some 550 feet across though, to be sure, it was in flood.

Much shaken by our passage beneath the previous bridges, we were already at a nervous disadvantage as we approached the *Pont de la Boverie* and I saw too that the step was more pronounced than ever. The four arches of this bridge all looked equally difficult to manoeuvre. In theory the right hand arch should have had the least current owing to the bend in the river, but as we came closer I could see that repairs were causing an obstruction and at the last moment I had to alter course. This caused us to lose our pathetic stock of speed and, as the bows reached the far side of the bridge, we were doing no more than holding our ground. For an eternity our fate hung in the balance and for the rest of my life I shall be able to see the view from the wheel-house window—the pointed front of the piers cleaving the brown depths of the Meuse, those foaming, turgid waters racing past, down to the detail of the cracks in the mortar between the stones of the arch.

I opened the throttle full. This usually had the effect of making the engine cough, but sometimes it would give an extra burst of power before giving up altogether; it did on this occasion. We mounted the step, emerged from the bridge and with what remained of our presence of mind began to look about for a mooring. Just ahead was a low quay with a small harbour. We steered across and tied up just as the engine lost power. I have never been more relieved to step ashore. If the engine had stopped and the anchor failed, what would have happened? Would we have been swept down the river and out into the North Sea some two days later, or would we have been poured over a weir and capsized? Whatever the nature of the fate that had so nearly been ours, to venture further without a better engine would be a clear invitation to disaster. This was it then: the end of our first journey. We had been remarkably lucky.

But now we should have to find a shipyard and make laborious and expensive arrangements for the replacement of the motor.

The row of drab houses ranged along the waterfront completed our depression; even the reflection in the water of the 'hundred steeples of Liège', hinting at its former distinction as an Episcopal city, did nothing to lift it. Robert Southey, visiting Liège all of one hundred and fifty years ago, had been no kinder than we in his judgement on the town, though for what seemed to us an enviably trivial reason. 'The church bells,' he complains 'were very loud, frequent and troublesome—this annoyance alone would have told us that we were in a Catholic country.'

If the church bells were a source of irritation, Southey at least would have been spared engine trouble for in those days, according to his own description, boats were pulled along the uncanalised river by horses walking along the river bed itself, the sides of the river being too shallow to allow towing from the bank. We ourselves could have made good use of the spare horse which it was customary to carry on board lest its working colleague should lose its footing on the uneven bottom and suffer injury or drowning.

H

10

Tarred but not feathered

We had landed at the Royal Yacht Club quay and the caretaker informed us that the offices of the Administration of the Meuse were just across the street. A junior official listened sympathetically while we explained our plight. Some of his colleagues soon arrived at his office in answer to his telephone call. The extent of their concern for our welfare encouraged us greatly and it was not long before we had been given several addresses to visit. The friend of a brother-in-law, the cousin of a wife, the nephew of the manager of the department—all would be in a position to help us. Yes, it would be folly to continue. The river was in flood and would take at least three days to go down. But why worry? The necessary introductions had been made and we should soon be fixed up.

With a lighter heart I set off in search of the friend of the brother-in-law who 'owned the largest ship's chandlery in Liège'; he would put us in touch with the 'leading supplier of diesel engines' and with the 'best shipyard', as he 'knew the owner personally'. We picked our way through a maze of dingy streets in a flurry of fine snow. At length we managed to pinpoint 'the largest ship's chandlery in Liège'.

My heart sank at the prospect of discussing a matter of such importance with a man in such a small way of business. His narrow, one-roomed shop offered for sale a small range of outboard motors and very little else. The man was out but an appointment was made through his wife for two o'clock, aboard the *Virginia Anne*.

Just as we were leaving, the telephone rang and our friends at the Administration told me of other appointments they had made for us. By the time I left the shop, I was committed to a full afternoon's programme. The wife was at great pains to explain that, despite the size of the shop, her husband was 'up and coming' and that the business was really much brisker than it appeared, various outside activities such as fitting engines in barges contributing to its size without being reflected in the dimensions of the premises. Certainly everyone was extremely friendly and, to celebrate our luck in having fallen into such willing hands, we purchased the ingredients for a specially good lunch.

It was during lunch that it began to dawn upon me that I was being led as a lamb to the slaughter. Could it be that these men, who had given so unstintingly of their advice and telephonic skill, were in reality motivated by thoughts of a sizeable commission? Could it be that I had fallen into the hands of some small men on the lookout for a quick profit out of an unsuspecting foreigner in potentially expensive trouble?

The more I relived the events of the morning and reflected on the glibness with which the whole operation had been conducted, the more certain I became that this was in fact the case. The feeling that 'an engine in the boat is worth two in the yard' began to take hold, together with a vast disenchantment with Liège. Quite illogically the flooded river assumed a steadily less formidable aspect as we proceeded with our excellent lunch. We speculated on the possibility of a 'do-it-yourself' repair to the engine and the prospects of a limited success seemed not unreasonable. As we were discussing it, a small band of men appeared at the top of the steps leading down to the far end of the quay.

On a sudden impulse we decided to go. The engine, in a final bid to save itself, cooperated and with a roar we cast off and headed upstream. A cloud of blue smoke from the engine-room enveloped the approaching sharks of Liège and they were lost to sight.

The city looked as uninviting as any in northern England and we were not sorry to be leaving. Although the weather probably played a significant part in producing depression and although the Liègeois whom we had met may not have been representative of the inhabitants, it is nonetheless a town to which I hope never to return. As we moved slowly toward the western limit of the city we passed, in the words of an ancient guide book 'the numerous chimneys which bear testimony to the industry of the artisans whose quarters are to be found amongst them'. We did not envy them, nor any of the other inhabitants, and we were not surprised to see many manifestations of political agitation. Car-borne travellers through Europe not unnaturally remain ignorant of the political slogans and counter-slogans painted on the underside of river bridges. These form a useful commentary on current issues and, as we were often in trouble and with time on our hands in just such places, we were in a position to study them at leisure.

Very gradually the current became less swift and as hour succeeded hour we began to make some useful progress on the map. Huge factories lined the banks and from the chimneys of each blew immense clouds of smoke that, having risen a short way, were caught by the prevailing wind and wafted east to hang like a pall over Liège. Foundries, cement factories and gas-works contributed plumes of smoke varying in shade from rich copper to charcoal, into which a jet of escaping steam would cut with dazzling whiteness. Numerous rivulets of polluted water poured into the river. For several hours factories, mines and quarries lined both banks in uninterrupted succession; never can any valley have been so ruined. Little by little the sides began to close in and to gain height and at intervals the cliffs were capped with the remains of a ruined castle. The neo-classical façades of the châteaux of the 19th century *nouveaux riches* bore witness against the promoters of the surrounding spoilation. It was not until Huy that we left the factories behind and the Meuse set itself up as a serious scenic rival to the Rhine. It was in fact the turning point: from this moment on the scenery remained as delightful as it had been depressing thus far.

The aspect of Huy from the river is very romantic. Behind the long quay a row of rather English-looking early Victorian houses hides a tangle of narrow, winding streets and gives the town a residential character. Overshadowing the houses along the front, the beautiful, immense Gothic church is itself dwarfed by the citadel which crowns the towering cliff behind the town. This fortress was used as a political prison by the Germans in World War II and some 700 inmates were murdered there. Awareness of this cruelty permeates the otherwise attractive town with a dark sadness and it is not a place in which to linger.

Occasional passenger boats run from Namur, further upstream, to Huy and downstream to Liège, but there is no organised service. Indeed, with the river in flood we found that we had moored directly above the quayside seats reserved for the summer excursionists. This became apparent only when the rudder fouled one on leaving.

Since Liège the engine had behaved impeccably, but my confidence was badly shaken by its past performance and there was every indication that the span of its natural life was nearly completed. Besides requiring a gallon of petrol for each mile, it was using about a pint of oil over the same distance; water leaked from various cracks around the engine block and a fountain spurted from the water pump. But there was no shipyard at Huy, nor did anyone know where such repairs could be undertaken other than at Liège. Namur, the next large town upstream, was mentioned as being a possible place.

After dinner I managed to find out the name of the secretary of a yacht club in Namur. Considerably later I discovered his telephone number and by the time I was connected, this excellent man was sound asleep. However he was soon awake and dealt efficiently and politely with my enquiry, giving the impression that it was perfectly normal for his sleep to be interrupted at this hour with such a question.

There was a great commotion in the town. A 500 ton barge coming downstream in the dark had collided with a 1,000 ton barge going upstream and the smaller boat had sunk. It lay across the bed of the river just ahead of us. Its crew of five had just escaped in time, but the dog had been drowned.

Next morning we passed the sunken barge; only the beflagged mast and the roof of the wheel-house protruded.

The first locks above Liège, part of the 2,000 ton system, had been formidable feats of engineering, entirely controlled electrically with closed-circuit television; we had been called forward through a loudspeaker as soon as the gates opened. But further upstream the older locks were still in use. Entry into several of these was complicated by

View from the wheelhouse window

a weir running parallel to the lock cut. Not only was there a considerable stream of water flowing down the lock cut; there were some unlikely currents to contend with as well. The effect of these can be to carry vessels of fairly shallow draught beneath the weir, an adventure that they do not survive.

By the time I had registered the position, we were uncomfortably near the fall and only narrowly missed being drawn into it.

It was in one of these smaller locks that we suffered the indignity of becoming stuck to another barge. The edge of our gunwale fender had somehow overlapped that of our neighbour. No one had noticed at the time and I was surprised to find that we were leaving the lock with more than customary speed and this without even having restarted the engine. The barge to which we clung belonged to an exceptionally dour man who was unable to derive any amusement from this unusual situation. He was unwilling to go astern and thereby risk falling behind us and he was every bit as unwilling to carry us as a passenger to the next lock. Although the tongue was unfamiliar, the tone of the remarks coming from his wheel-house was quite clear. I started the engine in case we should come apart and moved the wheel feebly from side to side in an effort to pacify him. We remained firmly clasped together. Increasingly desperate, he made as though to board our ship but, not wishing to leave his own wheel-house unattended, hestitated. The novelty of the situation was beginning to wear thin and we had determined to cooperate when our neighbour put into effect a most sinister manoeuvre.

His barge was heavier and more powerful than ours and

this gave him the idea of pushing us toward the bank and running us aground. The depth meter showed a gradual reduction in depth from eight feet below the keel to two as we closed in toward the bank. However it was a situation which, though unpleasant, was not uninteresting, for we could afford to sail much nearer the edge than could our neighbour, whose barge was laden. He dared not draw any closer and after half a mile or so gave up trying. We did not at all relish the idea of arriving at the next lock with a man half crazy with rage and managed, by a combination of full wheel and full astern, to pull apart.

———————

At the next lock we fell into conversation with a Dutch family on the boat next to ours. The skipper looked into the engine-room of the *Virginia Anne* and was clearly horrified. We put the blame for the chaos onto the engine, but he was not impressed and could hardly wait for a chance to show us his.

The machine-room of a 600 ton barge is a fairly large place—perhaps some 20 feet long—and a large proportion of this space is taken up with the engine itself which stands about as high as a man. The auxiliary machinery—pumps, generators, tanks and so on—occupy most of the remaining space. One would expect such an array of machinery to produce a fair amount of waste oil and dirt even if it were the subject of constant maintenance. However, since we had been invited to inspect it, we were prepared for our neighbour's engine-room to be spotless. The reality far exceeded my expectations; it was so clean that food could readily have been eaten off engine or floor alike. It was cleaner than a museum exhibit; unbelievably clean. As we left I caught sight of the daughter removing the marks left by our apparently dirty shoes. I subsequently discovered that this cleanliness was by no means exceptional for a barge and quite normal for a Dutch one.

In England the term 'to live like a bargee' is not intended as a compliment and is certainly not indicative of a scrupulous regard for hygiene. But the barges we saw were, with very few exceptions, quite extraordinarily free from dirt. In fact cleanliness is a mania. It is quite common for one of a crew of three to be permanently on deck cleaning or painting, and not only during periods in dock; deck-scrubbing and hosing are day-long tasks carried out even in the rain. Shoes and clogs are always removed before entering the living accommodation. And, as though decorated with flags, every other barge has a long line of washing strung from one end to the other, a useful guide to the size and composition of the family.

A great deal of competition is evident in the display of potted plants. They ornament the living-room windows of every 'self-respecting barge and their variety and colour appear to determine the status of the owner.

———————

The shipyard to which we were now bound was situated just before Namur. During the last few miles of our journey, tall cliffs of white limestone had dominated the scenery. From one of these cliffs at Marche-les-Dames, King Albert fell to his death and a cross commemorates the place of his fall.

The manner of our arrival at the shipyard was unusual. It had been uppermost in my mind that, in negotiating the price of a new engine, it would be most helpful to my cause if the extremity of our position could remain unappreciated. I was keen at all costs to preserve an air of little more than casual interest, and to this end I resolved to give the impression that we could just as easily call in here as at any shipyard this side of Lyon. Clearly, it would not help if my arrival were preceded by a pall of blue smoke and bursts of coughing.

Motivated then by these considerations, I decided to moor half a mile downstream, launch the dinghy and with the aid of the outboard motor arrive at the yard's quay with an air of nonchalance. Then I could open negotiations from a position of detachment, like a man seeking an overdraft who first convinces his bank manager that he doesn't really need the money anyhow.

We launched the dinghy with the usual difficulties and secured it with a line to the stern of the barge. The outboard motor was fetched up from the engine-room and fixed to the dinghy. Quite inexperienced in the operation of this motor, I sat in the rear of the dinghy interpreting the manufacturer's instructions step by step. Step number eleven involved pulling a lever smartly forward. To my great astonishment the engine instantly burst into frenzied activity, the dinghy leapt forward and—still secured to the barge—we described a tight half-circle and struck the side of the barge with a prodigious jolt. By the time we had picked ourselves up, the dinghy was off again, its line broken, snaking its way across the swollen Meuse and lurching violently from side to side, emitting hysterical screams. Everyone, much shaken, clutched desperately to the sides. With one hand on the tiller I was struggling to locate in the instruction leaflet step number twelve which might suggest a way of extinguishing life from this terrifying gadget. Unfortunately, at the moment of impact with the barge, the book had dropped into the partly water-filled dinghy and now the pages had stuck together, making it impossible to obtain one-handed the necessary information. Tentatively I moved a lever to one side and, as though stung by a gadfly, the boat bounded forward with a screeching whine. The handle on the tiller chose just this moment to fall off and I was reduced to trying to steer with the stub end only; protruding a mere two inches from the incandescent cylinder, the slightest movement set off a near right-angle turn and at every corner we shipped water. Our demented course was beginning to tell on our nerves as, with frozen masks of horror, we held our breath before the murky swirlings of the turgid Meuse.

We were by now nearing the shipyard and our latest convulsion had brought us alongside one of a row of several barges moored just before the quay. I was just about to take avoiding action when without warning the engine stopped as though it had been shot, an action I would willingly have performed had I possessed a gun. An incredible quietness suddenly prevailed. The force of the current counteracted our speed and we drifted into the side of the barge.

In an attempt to avoid being swept helplessly downstream, we tried to clutch the scarcely projecting rounded rivets of this steep-sided barge. The attempt was not entirely futile: the barge had just been tarred and our hands stuck resolutely to the sides. We found that by spreading our hands flat against the sticky surface we could cling like flies to a wall. But it was not so easy to detach a hand once glued, and many of our efforts in this direction nearly capsized us. With glacial slowness we worked our way up the inexhaustible length of the barge toward the bow and set out for the bank via the bows of the other barges moored in line abreast. The full horror struck as we reached the stern of the first barge: between the bows of the first and second barge the fierce current was constricted until it reached the point where the sides of the two barges met; the water boiled and frothed and whirled like Charybdis itself.

Balanced on the very front of the first barge and pressed

against this fulcrum by the force of the water, we dared move neither forward nor backward. We were becoming exhausted by the effort of maintaining the balance of this precarious position and it seemed only a matter of time before we lost hold and were swept away. All at once I became aware of shouts. A man was waving from a barge moored a hundred yards further upstream. Others joined him. A lifebelt on the end of a long line was thrown out into the river and, by jerks, guided to the side of the dinghy. We followed instructions to tie the end to the dinghy and were finally pulled up beneath the side of the barge. A ladder was lowered and with shaking knees we sheepishly climbed aboard. We were black with tar and soaked to the skin. Our nerves were shattered and we felt extremely foolish. Everyone had stopped work to observe our escape from drowning. The manager of the yard introduced himself.

These were not exactly the circumstances in which I had visualised my arrival to open negotiations. I suspected that my position had been severely compromised. And rightly. It was a Saturday morning, the yard would be closing for the weekend in a quarter of an hour and I had to return to England the following day. The manager was clearly unimpressed by my appearance and seemed not to take my enquiry seriously. He was not in any case prepared to give an opinion without first seeing the boat, but he did finally agree to stay at the yard while we fetched it.

This was easier said than done, but within an hour I had the barge alongside and disembarked to find the manager. The yard appeared entirely deserted and all the offices were locked up. I felt extremely angry, my anger being divided fairly equally against myself and the yard manager. In a desultory manner I started wandering about the yard; there were huge 1,500 ton barges hauled up on to blocks at the top of the bank, one or two new barges under construction and a two-tiered pleasure steamer from the last century. Then I saw smoke coming from the galley chimney of one of the barges on blocks and realised that the bargees still lived aboard them and no doubt knew where the manager lived.

The hapless manager was eventually unearthed. By this time I had been able to smarten up my appearance and, in an effort to redress the balance, I assumed the imperious attitude of one who, if not given prompt and satisfactory service, would not hesitate to buy up the entire yard and replace the management. Although the condition of my vessel did not exactly lend weight to my act, a considerable amount of attention was forthcoming and by evening satisfactory arrangements had been concluded in all matters excepting the actual choice of engine. This was obviously a subject of great importance and not one to be decided in total ignorance. I made up my mind to consult a number of bargees and obtain advice, delaying the decision until the following morning.

We spent that evening at the local café which was taken over almost entirely by bargees and yard workers. As though by bush telegraph everyone seemed to know our business. A broad discussion on the relative merits of the various makes of diesel engine was in full swing and the exchanges were heated. Only we contributed nothing to the conversation and after an hour or so the café had virtually divided itself into two groups of supporters for the two most popular makes of engine. Feeling grew strong between the groups and tongues became sufficiently loosened by countless rounds of drinks to reveal some of the shortcomings of the yard and its staff. This information afterwards proved most helpful.

I subsequently discovered that some of the more sharp-witted contenders for this or that engine had availed themselves of the opportunity to slip out and telephone the local agent with a view to establishing themselves in line for commission. When I had finally made up my mind and placed the order with the yard, I received invoices for the engine from no less than three agents, all of whom hoped to get in on the act.

I abandoned the *Virginia Anne* to her temporary home. I might—such was the sadness I felt—have been leaving my dog at a strange kennel.

I I

Virginia Anne meets Virginia Anne

The ensuing weeks were punctuated by letters announcing unforeseen difficulties. Prominent amongst these was the problem of lowering the new engine through the engine-room hatch which was only half the requisite size. Such allegedly unpredictable setbacks prolonged the work and I grew impatient for completion.

One hot evening in May, my wife and I arrived at Namur station and took a taxi the few miles to the shipyard. Everything had changed. There were very few barges in for repair and the Meuse had shrunk from a wide, foaming torrent to a placid river many feet lower than when I had last seen it. An exciting smell of tar drifted on the warm air as we crossed the yard. A large brown rat scurried away toward a pile of timber. Two men were hammering the rudder of a barge while a third painted some new work in vivid orange.

It was my wife's first visit to the ship named after her

and I was anxious that she should not be disappointed. We peered over the bank, but the *Virginia Anne* was not amongst the half-dozen large barges lying there. Could it be that she was still ashore on blocks? With sinking hearts we made a quick tour of the yard; there was no sign of her. Perhaps she had been taken out on trials? Not at this hour, surely, and in any case she was not sufficiently completed. Could she have been stolen? An immense feeling of anti-climax swept over us and we sat on a concrete block to take stock of the position. Then suddenly my wife noticed a mast projecting above and between the sides of two barges, apparently belonging to neither. We scrambled across the gangway and over the two intervening barges and there, looking ridiculously small, lay our boat, sandwiched between two huge thousand tonners.

The deck was black with oil. Huge pieces of engine lay scattered over the boat like entrails over a battle-field—steel plates, pipes, assorted tools, oxygen cylinders, drums of fuel. Chaos was complete and we speculated that it would take days and days to finish the work. Had I set about it the wrong way and overlooked the question of incentive? Robert Louis Stevenson, beset with similar troubles during a canoe journey in France, speaks of 'the amount of sweet champagne consumed in the inn at the bridge end, to give zeal to the workmen and speed to the work'. It was too late for such thoughts now.

By the end of the day a great deal of progress had been made and, incredibly, the following afternoon we were ready for trials.

The new engine was a 125 horse-power DAF diesel and, to utilise this increased power more efficiently, a new and larger propeller had been fitted. I could hardly wait to see the results. Some had predicted that it would make very little difference, others that the barge would now advance like an aquaplane. I had been prepared to settle for slightly

J

increased speed, reliability and long life.

The engine was started. It made a far happier sound than its predecessor (which I had actually managed to part-exchange for a fair sum, much to my surprise) and, apart from some unorthodox manoeuvring attributable to the fitting back-to-front of the Forward-Astern tele-control lever, it behaved well. As the engine could not be run at full speed at this stage, effective speed trials could not be conducted. Aquaplaning aside, however, it seemed reasonable to expect an extra knot or two.

In a flurry of handshakes, we bid farewell to the yard; they had indeed surpassed themselves in the hour of need.

With the usual mixed feelings of exhilaration and misgiving we set off up the river. Just round the first corner we were faced with a weir and lock. I had carefully drilled my wife in the art of jumping from ship to shore, disregarding both the distance and one's ugly fate in the event of falling between the two, and I considered her well trained. But as we approached the mooring bank before the lock, my wife stared with unconcealed horror at the yawning gap that, owing to the shelving bank, could never be closed. She failed to jump. Caught by the current, the bow began to swing out. As we lined ourselves up sideways before the weir, I put my entire trust in the new engine.

But I had reckoned without the new propeller, whose superior design ensured far greater acceleration. By the time I realised this, I was in danger of striking the opposite bank, lined at this point with a concrete wall. Hard astern, I watched the distance diminish too rapidly and found that the propeller was not effective astern. At this point my wife too realised the nature of our predicament;

with great determination she rushed to the bow and just before the crashing impact I saw her holding out a mop to fend off our 115 tons. We never saw the mop again.

Through the lock, we had decided to stay at Namur for the night, and were hoping to meet a friend there. Namur, so frequently disputed on account of its strategic position, is virtually a distillation of the whole of Belgium's spectacular history of one foreign conquest upon another.

Namur is at the junction of the Meuse, which we were to follow, and the Sambre,* main waterway to the Paris area. As in the case of the Meuse downstream of Namur, the Sambre is at present the subject of a large constructional programme to increase its carrying capacity from a nominal 300 tons to a projected 1,350 tons. At present the journey from Namur to Paris entails locking through some 85 locks, 23 of them on the Belgian side. The Sambre siphons off almost all the traffic upstream from Namur, so that from this point on—over literally thousands of miles of waterway subsequently travelled within the remainder of Belgium and France—we were never amongst heavy traffic and only rarely had to queue at a lock.

We had not foreseen the practical advantage of having a friend on the quayside, but in the event it proved very helpful. The entire quayside throughout the town was occupied, except for a single space. It was the best position in the town, right in front of the main square, and consequently our suspicions were vaguely aroused. We had to moor in a minimum of space just behind a small tourist excursion boat and this difficult manoeuvre was greatly facilitated by the presence of our quayside friend who was able to take the line and pull us in sideways. By the time we were moored it was nearly dark.

The following morning we noticed that the wall opposite

See Notes

was covered with instructions forbidding mooring under any circumstances. Having crossed the square to purchase stores, we returned to find some kind of town official in a state of indignation; we were occupying the space reserved for the town's main excursion boat. Indeed, already a young couple were asking to be taken up the river. We told them not to worry, for we would gladly take them the seven miles to Profondeville. The remonstrances of the officials were politely dismissed and the couple were delighted; they sat in the wheel-house, arms linked, gazing into each other's eyes during the entire journey. On disembarking, they insisted on pressing a handsome tip into my hand. I found I had little difficulty in allowing myself to accept and felt full of generous feelings towards the tourist organisation at Namur.

It was a radiant Sunday in late spring, and the Meuse could have been mistaken for the Chiltern Thames in the eighteen-nineties. Victorian villas with neatly-mown lawns were the back-cloth against which respectable family groups digested their lunches in the shade of weeping willows while the children and dogs ran restrained and respectful circles round their elders and betters. A number of drowsy, Sunday fishermen sat hunched in small boats along the river's edge casting a speculative eye at the likely effect of our wash on their floats. The impression of the past was reinforced by the sight of a punt being poled slowly downstream by a young man in a straw boater while his companion reclined gracefully on boat cushions, a brightly-coloured parasol shading her head.

The contrast with the Thames of today was striking. The Meuse would present a very different face if it had the misfortune to flow through England. The surface of the river would be criss-crossed with the wake of motor-boats making the area hideous with their noise; picnic parties would be deciding whether to abandon their rubbish altogether or to throw it into the river; the accessible banks would be lined with cars and motor-cycles; caravan and camping sites would destroy what was left of peace and sanity with the help of portable transistors. But here there were hardly any motor-boats and one almost felt that the river was unappreciated. We wondered whether our disturbing passage was resented but the waves of the bystanders reassured us.

Continuing south through several locks, the scenery improved all the way to Dinant, where we found an excellent and unopposed mooring beneath the great onion-domed Eglise Collégiale de Notre-Dame. The citadel of Montfort towered above us, taking our minds back again to the long history of the Meuse valley as a battlefield; Dinant in particular had a hand in every skirmish. One of any number of horrific incidents relating to Dinant occurred in 1466 when the Duke of Burgundy enjoying the name of Philip the Good pillaged and burned the town in revenge for the hanging in effigy of his son. Not content with this, he had eight hundred of the inhabitants bound together in pairs, back to back, and thrown into the Meuse.

The town that we see today dates largely from its rebuilding since 1914, the year in which it was last mercilessly sacked, this time by German invaders. It was too early in the season for the tourists to have invaded the town in their hordes, but the shops were fully stocked with the already stale gingerbread men and animals which, together with the ugly beaten copper ornaments, are the speciality of the town. We enjoyed sitting in the wheel-house eating our lunch in the warmth of the spring sunshine, watching the activity in the town square.

Dinant sheltering under its fortress

Soon after lunch we were again on our way upstream with a pronounced lack of concentration when we suddenly realised that we had missed the previous lock-cut and were heading straight for a weir. The sections of river between lock-cut and weir are of course never dredged and are therefore shallow and unpredictable. The problem was how to turn in a confined area and against a powerful stream. A number of people gathered to witness a possible grounding. Fortunately the current assisted and we turned with little help from the engine. Although uneventful, this experience taught us to keep a much sharper eye for lock-cuts in future. We had been lucky to get away with it.

When we arrived at the lock and were about to enter, we were waved back to make way for another barge appearing from behind. We immediately suspected bribery. Throwing a rope round a roadside post, I made fast and hurried toward the lock full of righteous indignation. I was about to protest to the lock-keeper when I saw that the offending barge was lined with soldiers. It was carrying 600 tons of explosives. It bore impressive notices proclaiming its rights of priority; indeed it also carried the triangular red flag at the bow that indicated just such a cargo. Earlier in Belgium I had hoisted this flag which, according to an English guide to the Belgian waterways, marked the priority accorded to private yachts. It had not been worn for long, as its appearance incited first curiosity and then understandable annoyance.

Every ship sailing the Meuse has to fly from the bow a large red rectangular flag with a white rectangle in the centre. This is the regulation. No one knows the reason for it, but Belgian officialdom has nevertheless succeeded in achieving almost total conformity on this point. I had removed both flag and staff earlier that day as a precaution against a particularly low bridge. Now we were subjected to a treatise from the lock-keeper on the importance of obeying rules in general and of flying the Meuse flag in particular. Still we failed to discover its purpose.

A little to the south of Dinant is the junction with the river Lesse. The Lesse is navigable over a short section and can be descended from Houyet in kayaks—a journey of some 20 kilometres, much to be recommended. During the summer months this section of river has a scheduled passenger service operating between the frontier and Dinant. The whole area is full of caves, and the cliffs—as we were shortly to become aware—are a favourite haunt of climbers.

We were progressing along the increasingly beautiful stretch of river near Waulsort and had slowed down to look at the charming old Benedictine abbey just before the village when there was a sudden, very loud bang from the engine-room. Seconds later a column of steam issued from the engine-room hatch. I stopped the engine at once and wondered what disaster could have overtaken this new installation. Meanwhile we drifted on engineless into a very conveniently-placed lock-cut where we brought ourselves to a halt in the lock by means of a slipping rope around a bollard.

In the engine-room there was water everywhere. The generator pulley wheel had flown off, causing the fan belt to become dislodged and the engine to overheat. I thought it would be the work of a minute or two to find the wheel, key and nut and effect the repair whilst we were being raised to the next level. But it was not as simple as I thought. Beneath the engine is a pool of liquid sludge which has accumulated in the bottom of the barge over rather more than half a century. By the time the locking had been completed I had, with the aid of a kitchen ladle,

Benedictine Abbey near Waulsort

found the pulley wheel itself, but finding the small nut and the even smaller key was quite another matter. The lock-keeper signalled us to leave, but to leave was impossible. I fetched a tray and with great speed embarked on the delightful task of sifting the sludge of ages. I came across many interesting items and nuts of all sizes, but not the one required. The lock-keeper was becoming impatient and it was only a matter of minutes before there was going to be a nasty scene. I searched even more furiously, overcoming my reluctance to use my hands. Miraculously the two pieces appeared, still coupled together, and it took no time to replace the wheel and belt. The lock-keeper had gone into his office by the time I came up and I heard him telephoning the news and presumably asking for instructions for our disposal.

The reach following this lock was incredibly beautiful. On the right hay-fields led up to a wooded slope, and on the left limestone cliffs rose sheer from the water's edge hundreds of feet to craggy summits. We could hear the shouts of climbers and could see far above us their tiny, spread-eagled figures motionless against the rock face. The surface of the river was quite still and it seemed vandalistic to disturb it. There was no other traffic whatsoever and we moored for the night at a point where the cliffs fell back a little from the water's edge. We wove an effective but un-seamanlike web of rope around some alders and hoped that the level of water would not change much in the course of the night.

We decided to have a short walk before dinner to see if we could find some lilies-of-the-valley, which grow plentifully in parts of the Belgian Ardennes. We had gone only a few hundred yards and were nearing the cliff where we had seen the climbers, when we heard a shout which was immediately followed by the arrival of a colossal boulder falling through the trees above us. It crashed mere feet away and exploded like a grenade. Neither of us was hit by the fragments, but it was enough to make us race for the comparative safety of the water and a bottled restorative.

12

Black hole of Ham

To awake in the morning and see a kingfisher flying past the window is a rare delight. Such is the nature of travel along the waterways. It is to relive the formative childhood years when new sights, sounds and scents impress themselves indelibly on the memory. Who could forget the sand martins skimming across the water beneath a slowly rising mist to announce yet another fine day; or the sound of a moorhen in the reeds at the water's edge; or the scent of the river itself, 'thrilling, sweet and rotten', as Rupert Brooke so exactly describes it? Drawing back the bedroom curtains in the morning is almost the only routine activity in the business of living which is so entirely delightful for the unhurried bargee. Certainly for us, the edge of our inexperience softened and the tension reduced, the days followed fast upon each other in a blur of happiness. In these days when subtle methods are devised to restrict individual choice, when even so personal a matter as the way in which one spends one's holiday is dictated—if not by fashion then by the travel agent with his package tour—we found our-

selves revelling in the tranquillity, the freedom, the informality.

We had just passed through a lock a little after midday one day and were still in the narrow lock cut when we smelt a particularly appetising aroma and traced it to a restaurant. Making a sudden decision to stop for lunch, we moved slowly toward a mooring. The *patron* himself came running over to take the end of the mooring line. Meanwhile the lock-keeper had realised our intention and seen the theoretical possibility of our obstructing the lock cut in this virtually deserted reach. He shouted to us to move on, advancing on the restaurant. The *patron* told us to take no notice and ushered us inside. No sooner had we sat down at our table than the inevitable altercation opened between the *patron* and the lock-keeper. I must confess that the sauce for the *côtes de porc ardennais* was rendered the more piquant by feelings of guilt.

The only drawback to an arrival at a restaurant by water is that by the time the staff have made fast the mooring ropes it is rather harder to take a casual glance at the menu, assess its worth and, should it be found wanting, make a getaway.

Scenically, the route of the *Virginia Anne* had improved steadily all the way from central Holland to the south-west of Belgium. And now, as we approached the Franco-Belgian border, we could not help wondering whether we might not be disappointed by the landscape beyond the frontier. Our apprehension increased as, with the last few miles of Belgian territory, the wooded hills receded into the background and development closed in toward the river. The Meuse broadened and seemed almost to have lost its current. It was strange to reflect that since we entered its fattened waters in the teeth of a winter's storm, not only had we watched as it grew tame and subdued but we had in the process almost imperceptibly climbed some three hundred and thirty feet. This represents nearly a third of the ascent across the land mass of the Continent. Our route to the south lay through the Vosges and there, some 110 locks further on, we would achieve the summit of the staircase across Europe, a respectable elevation of 1,200 feet or, by official English definition, 200 feet above the altitude at which a hill becomes a mountain. And, with a mental image of Noah's Ark grounding to a halt on Mount Ararat, I was jerked back to the present by a large notice 'DOUANES' and the sight of a long quay beyond.

The Belgian customs officers were bored and boring. Several itinerant vendors were lying in wait, hoping to trap us into the same purchases as those to which we had fallen victim at the hands of their colleagues on the other side of Belgium. We collected from a nearby garage four old motor tyres to replace those we had lost and moved on as quickly as possible toward the French customs two or three miles further on.

The customs' formalities for France were, we understood, carried out in Givet and as we arrived in the town we fell in behind an immense assemblage of barges moored in line abreast. Our hearts sank as we envisaged endless delays and queues. It was a Saturday morning and by the time we landed only a quarter of an hour remained before the Customs closed. I hurriedly scoured the quayside buildings for the Customs offices, but failed to locate them. Referred continually from one end to the other, after several passages I narrowed the area to a distance of a few yards. Still I could not see the buildings, nor any of the defensive architecture which normally isolates the premises of this fraternity. Then, as the town clock struck the hour, I noticed an ancient, uniformed man standing in the doorway of an apparently uninhabited house. Taking him for a postman, I asked him if he would kindly lead me to the Customs house. He expressed willingness but made no move. I asked again and with an unhurried wave of a rheumatic hand he indicated the building behind us. I asked if he would mind moving to one side as I wished to see the customs officer before the offices shut. Certainly, he replied, though the offices were officially shut by now. I entered a completely bare-walled and cramped room furnished with only a desk and chair. Nothing gave away its identity and only the presence of a few rubber stamps on the desk gave any impression of authenticity. The place was deserted. I waited, but no one came. The old postman was still leaning against the door and I sought his advice:

'Excuse me, can you please tell me where I can find the Customs Officer?'

'*M'sieur le Douannier? C'est moi,*' he replied, without conviction.

'*C'est vous?*'

'*C'est moi,*' he repeated with greater assurance and relapsed into silence.

'*S'il vous plaît, M'sieur, j'ai les papiers pour mon bateau,*' I said, proffering the documents.

'*Vous avez des papiers, M'sieur?*'

'*Oui, j'ai les papiers.*' A further silence followed and he gazed out wistfully toward the cool darkness beneath a giant horse chestnut tree. Leaning against the trunk was an antiquated bicycle and he looked from one of us to the other before his gaze came to rest on the ground.

'*Vous avez des papiers alors?*' he stirred himself at length.

'*Oui, j'ai les papiers,*' I said in as comforting a tone as possible, for he looked infinitely sad. The conversation seemed to be at an end.

'*Le bureau est fermé,*' he said after another long pause,

K

still torn between his tiny office and his waiting bicycle. *'Voyez-vous, ma femme m'attend pour déjeuner.'*

'Je regrette . . .,' I began, but he interrupted me.

'Je reviendrai dans une demi-heure pour timbrer vos papiers.' I thanked him profusely as, with a look of resignation to the endless demands of politeness, he mounted his tall bicycle and rode unsteadily off.

During the ensuing half hour I found myself making wildly partisan comparisons between Dutch officialdom and French, the latter being for the moment wholly personified by this gentle, good-natured old man. True to his word, he returned punctually and took possession of the papers. He assumed an air of immense anxiety as he studied them. Amongst them were probably many with which he was not familiar. Before setting out on the voyage, I had with some difficulty obtained a letter from the French Ministry of Finance exempting the *Virginia Anne* from the statutory payment of duty after a six-months sojourn in the country and I had a letter which had been sent from the *Quai d'Orsay* advising the Givet Customs post of my intended passage. By way of encouragement I selected this document from amongst the others and drew it to his attention. But he appeared not to take it in, all his energies being concentrated on the completion of the form dealing with the importation of oil. He became obsessed with the desire to know exactly how much oil, down to the last litre, we were carrying and even asked to be allowed to count for himself the extent of our stocks. I left him to make his own calculations, which he did at length, apparently including the oil in the oil-can. Then he handed back the papers and wished us a pleasant journey.

We moved on to the other end of the town and moored for the night before an attractive square. 'Nothing of interest for the tourist', is Baedeker's somewhat summary pronouncement on the town. High above us the immense fortress of Charlemont marked the start of a tall cliff forming the right bank of the river beyond Givet.

The sight of our red ensign attracted, as usual, a circle of curious onlookers. It was Saturday evening and the town was crowded with soldiers from the local garrison and the families of dozens of bargees. We wondered at the size of the small fleet of barges that had chosen to tie up here. We turned Givet into the spearhead of a vast smuggling network, bargees and Customs men engaged in a desperate battle of wits. In fact we had to admit that Givet was probably simply a diverting place in which to spend the weekend.

Having celebrated our arrival in France over-zealously, we were late in making a start the following morning. When I eventually did emerge on deck, I was astonished to find the Customs official of the previous evening standing patiently beside the gangplank. He looked genuinely relieved to see me and I wondered what error or omission could have brought him to us. The capping and honeyed phrases dispensed with, all he apparently wanted was to know whether or not he had signed our copy of the oil declaration so painstakingly completed.

As we continued upstream I was struck again by the remarkable change of atmosphere on entering France; not just the altered physiognomy of people and landscape but a meteorological phenomenon—that special luminosity which distinguishes northern France from anywhere else in the world. By contrast bordering countries are seen through a slightly darkened lens. Unconnected with the weather, it is an inherent characteristic and one which the French Impressionists of course knew well. Accompanying this transformation was the less subtle change of architectural style and of the hundred and one elements that go to make up a country's individuality. It always seems uncanny that an artificially contrived frontier can be such an effective dividing line. No sooner had I crossed this one than I marvelled, as I always do, at the timelessness and immutability so quintessential to France, a land with a soul of its own.

Before long we arrived at the lock heralding the entrance to the *Souterrain de Ham,* a tunnel nearly half a mile long (565 metres) whose theoretical dimensions almost exactly balanced those of the *Virginia Anne.* The lock was closed as we drew near, so we prepared to moor alongside a barge that was already tied up to the bank. We bargained without the very strong and sudden gust of wind that blew us into the side of this other boat. The owner and his large family were just settling down to the Sunday *déjeuner,* a ritual sacred in France, when they received the impact of our arrival. They poured out of the wheel-house in an apparently endless stream: red-faced father, enormous mother and children in assorted sizes. I was offering profuse apologies in my inadequate French when suddenly a loud explosion sounded from a nearby quarry, creating a welcome diversion. With a shout of panic, the entire family fought to get inside the wheel-house, pouring out again only when the stones had stopped falling. Deprived of dignity and the advantage of a sudden counter-attack, the father tempered his observations with a good deal of restraint.

The lock gates opened and a barge, considerably lower than ours, shuffled its way out. I could see the inside of the tunnel now and the chances of our being able to get through so small an aperture looked remote.

The lock-keeper, replete after his Sunday lunch and filled with benevolence toward us, joined in our conversation.

On hearing the height of the boat, a shower of exclamations burst from him like splinters from a smashed sheet of glass.

'*Mais ça ira ou ça n'ira pas?*' I asked with objective persistence, but he was not to be drawn. The description he made with his arms of the knife-edge precariousness of the position was eloquent enough.

'*Peut-être que oui; peut-être que non. Il faut bien tenir le centre.*'

'*Bien tenir le centre*', chorused the rest of his family, adding their piece to the suspense of the drama.

Finally it had to be admitted that even if the wheel-house would pass, the chimney certainly would not and must be dismantled. The tunnel was unlined and the jagged rock would probably damage the wheel-house roof. The constant buffetings of the barges' iron sides had over the years made the sides relatively smooth, but the roof was another matter. We must understand that all the other barges were lower, being laden, and their owners highly skilled. Oh, and just one other thing, they felt they should add: there was no tow-path through the tunnel and if we did become impaled on the jagged roof they could not see how we should ever get out.

The black hole could not have had a more sinister aspect and the pinhole of light at the far end might have belonged to another planet. We looked about us. With that heightened sense of perception of people about to be deprived of liberty, I could have sworn that the flowers in the grass became instantly brighter and the sun warmer; the sky turned a deeper blue as I watched and the scent of the hay had never been so intoxicating.

Across the river a rather new looking château, planted around with immature trees, caught my attention. Anxious

to postpone our impending departure, I asked the lock-keeper about it. He cast a pitying look toward the house and explained that it was occupied by a Belgian government minister who normally only used it at weekends. '*M'sieur le Ministre*, he walks about all day with a serious expression on his face, arms behind his back, dressed in a dark suit,' and he assumed an expression of deepest melancholy as he paced up and down the edge of the lock, lending to the unhappy minister a ludicrous image. 'The Belgians,' he went on, 'they are all the same. They spend all their life waiting to die. They do not know how to live!' and he dismissed them with a scornful shrug of the shoulders.

'*Alors, au tunnel!*' he said happily, waving to us to be on our way. '*Bonne chance!*', '*Tenez le centre!*' and '*Doucement!*' followed us as we inched our way toward the forbidding entrance. The bows passed smoothly beneath the arched façade and were lost to sight in the ebon interior. Gradually the length of the barge was swallowed up until the wheel-house too had entered its jaw. Just before all vision was lost in the sudden change from full sunlight to almost total obscurity, I was able to see that even when we kept to dead centre, there was no more than a foot's clearance between the sides of the wheel-house roof and the vault of the tunnel.

I switched on the searchlight and wished I hadn't. The rounded top of the tunnel was a mass of pointed rock, green, slimy and dripping. The engine made a deafening din and in an abandoned moment I could not resist the temptation of experimenting with the horn. The roar filled me with terror and resounded throughout our dungeon. I felt convinced that the roof would collapse and spent anxious moments in an orgy of self-criticism. Looking back after what seemed like hours, I was appalled to find that we had progressed only forty or fifty yards. Below two knots, a barge has very little steerage and at the speed of under half a knot which we were now making it has virtually none. It is just possible to alter course through skilful use of engine and rudder, but this is easier done other than in a dark tunnel where it is impossible to see the position of the rudder indicator.

Having proceeded with great patience for rather more than half the length, I consoled myself with the thought that I too must have acquired some skill to have kept to the centre with such exactitude. Solace was shortlived. Almost at once I realised that the bows were slightly left of centre. In my anxiety to avoid a particularly vicious rock, I delayed moving the stern across just too long. I would now have to steer more violently to extricate the bows from their collision course, but if I strayed more than a few inches from the centre line the wheel-house roof would strike the top. I attempted a hopeless compromise. A loud crash a foot or so above my head exploded upon the silence as the wheel-house roof struck solid rock. There was a rending sound as the entire upper half of the wheel-house tilted backwards; planks were torn from the roof and I was showered with dust carefully preserved over decades.

I felt sick with annoyance and half-expected at any minute to be brushed beneath the collapsing roof. Just before the impact I had put the engine full astern and, combined with the stopping force of the crash, this had brought us to a halt. I surveyed the damage briefly and with mounting claustrophobia started off again for the exit. This time my wife stood on the after-deck pushing with a broom against the slimy sides of the tunnel in an effort to keep us straight. We emerged without further incident. The brilliance of the sun and the sudden warmth were such that we might have escaped from a tomb. In the event we counted ourselves lucky to have escaped so lightly. For if the outcome of such a tunnel journey seemed to border on the haphazard, it had to be remembered that in the days of horse-drawn barges, tunnels without towpaths had to be manipulated by 'leggers' as they were called—teams of men lying on their backs on the roof of the hold, 'treading' the tunnel vault like some monstrous overturned insect. But then, in the course of the last century, certain tunnels had been equipped with chains which were laid along the canal bed and which the barges could haul in ahead and drop out astern. A similar system was employed in the Harecastle tunnel on the Trent & Mersey, where the electric tug worked on a chain. This system may also be seen working in the tunnel at Pouilly-en-Auxois on the Burgundy Canal. Recently experiments have been made in France with electric tractors suspended from a monorail.

Outside was a barge impatiently waiting to enter the tunnel, apparently having been held up for some time while we passed. The owner shouted something which I did not understand but which I took to relate to the nature of my parentage. I absent-mindedly nodded my agreement with whatever his observation might have been and he started off into the tunnel without further exchange. No sooner had he gone than I realised that he had probably asked me whether or not he was free to pass and I remembered too late that the man I had bumped into before entering the previous lock was next. Someone would have to go back. I did not wait to see who it would be.

Our apprehension as to the scenery ahead had been unfounded. Within a few miles of the frontier we were again in enchanting surroundings. Here the Ardennes were perhaps less dramatic than on the Belgian side but I thought them more beautiful. Steeply wooded slopes rose some five hundred feet above us, but they were rounded hills, set back from the river and often separated from the bank by hay-fields. It was intensely peaceful. There was next to no traffic, perhaps two or three barges a day and the occasional fisherman's punt. We passed a few inactive villages where even the cafés were quiet. Occasionally, when the road neared the river, we would see the figure of a mid-twentieth century motorist huddled over the wheel of his car and count ourselves lucky.

Lulled into a mood of deep tranquillity by the loveliness of the countryside and drugged by the heat of the sun, we decided to take it in turns to lie on a deck-bed in a sheltered spot on the fore-deck. I went below and fetched it, unfolded it and placed it in a carefully sited position out of the breeze. I could hardly wait to have my turn of luxurious idleness and it required some effort of mind to offer it first to my wife. Up at the bow, when in progress, one can hear only the sound of the bow-wave lapping the sides; watching the passing scene from this position is the nearest thing to travelling on a magic carpet. The prospect was therefore, as I have said, enchanting and I despatched my wife without loss of time in order that my turn would come the sooner.

'Where's the bed?' she yelled as soon as she reached the foredeck.

'What do you mean, where's the bed?' I shouted back, irritated by the pointlessness of the question. But the bed had vanished. It had been blown overboard by a sudden gust and had sunk without trace.

There is a great deal of skill to be acquired in reaching a lock and finding it open. Although this depends to some extent on the timing of barges coming in the opposite direc-

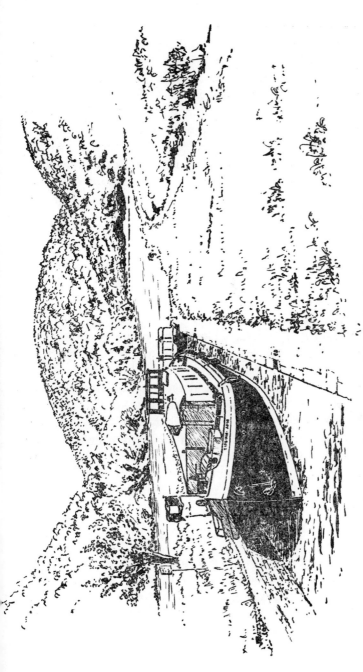

A peaceful lock on the Meuse in the French Ardennes

tion, the correct psychological treatment of the lock-keeper plays an important part. The probability is that when not operating the lock, he will either be attending to the cultivation of his vegetable garden, feeding his chickens or sitting in the shade of the fruit tree which is provided as part of his statutory equipment, gently dozing in the company of his ancient dog. Many lock-keepers are *blessés de guerre* enjoying a semi-retirement and of all the excellent qualities for which they are renowned, speed cannot be counted amongst them. It is therefore important to advertise one's impending arrival in good time to avoid the bother of mooring, and this is done by means of the ship's horn.

This would be simple enough were it not complicated by the fact that a good many lock-keepers are somewhat deaf. One cannot of course know in advance which are deaf and which are not—a printed guide would be worth gold—and an unusually strident blast carried on a following wind will give offence to a sensitive ear and the offender be kept waiting twice as long. Moreover, the *Virginia Anne* travels faster than other barges and even cooperative lock-keepers tend to leave the opening of the gate until too late. This means hanging around for several minutes at the entrance to a lock cut, where as often as not one loses one's carefully prepared alignment, the current of the river flowing at an angle against the hull. And, with mere inches to spare on either side, positioning is all-important.

We had decided to stay a night at Fumay, partly because it fitted in with the timing of our arrival and partly because some seven years before we had stayed at an hotel at nearby Haybes where we had eaten memorable quantities of the excellent local *jambon cru*.

But just before we stopped, our attention was caught by the sight of the stern of a 600 ton barge projecting out of the river at a steep angle. There appeared to be no one aboard and we made enquiries at the next lock. Apparently the barge had been moored just below the lock when in the middle of the night the ropes had broken and it had drifted down with the current without the bargees having awoken. At two o'clock in the morning it had struck a rock and sunk just above a weir, avoiding total disaster by only a few feet. At this point the bargees awoke to find themselves under water. Too frightened to attempt swimming to the shore, fortunately the rear water-tight compartment held and they were able to stay inside their bathysphere until they were rescued at daybreak.

Fumay presents an attractive front to the river, across a wide strip of rough grass. Any bollards there may have been were concealed by this long grass, so we kept an eye out for a passer-by who could locate one and slip the rope over it. We did not have long to wait before we spotted a strong-looking young man standing idly by the bank. We called to him and threw the end of the line for him to catch, bringing the barge in alongside. He seemed to understand what was required of him and, not waiting to see the job completed, I went down to the engine room to turn off everything for the night. My wife was attending to the mooring of the stern. When I emerged from the hatch I was amazed to see that our recruit, having pulled in as much of the line as he could—well over 100 feet—had coiled the entire length round and round the bollard until it looked like a spool of rope. He came to the end of the line as I watched. Sitting down, he continued to pull at the end, enjoying a secret joke. We had of course managed to single out the village idiot and once with us he would not leave.

Since the collision in the tunnel, despite much effort applied to straightening it, the wheel-house would not lock.

Obviously if we were to stay at Fumay and in the vicinity of our new acquaintance, it would be wise to lock everything up as securely as possible, so I thought I should try to complete restoration of the upper part of the wheelhouse. I had an idea: by tying a rope round the top, just beneath the roof, and placing the other end on the winch on the fore-deck, I might be able to pull it forward. I succeeded to some extent, but more tension was needed than I could provide by turning the winch handle. Ah, but if I could persuade our new friend to hang on to the rope in front of the wheel-house, this would provide a considerably increased pull. I gave a demonstration of what I intended and he followed suit. He succeeded in wrapping himself round the rope, hanging like a monkey, and he remained in this position chuckling to himself, thrilled with the part he was playing and keeping a watchful eye on the bank to see how large an audience he was attracting. It was quite another matter persuading him to come down again and in the end I had to release the ratchet on the winch, causing him a rather sudden landing. Nevertheless the wheel-house was now more or less straight again. We locked up and set off in search of the restaurant, only to find that it had closed the previous year.

The following morning our star plunged deep into the descendent. We were ready to leave, mooring ropes removed and engine started. I moved the control lever into forward position. In response there was a very loud thud and the deck began to vibrate violently. The propeller had fouled something and one of the blades had broken off.

This was obviously a major setback and I telephoned the shipyard at Namur for advice. I felt very slightly less grieved about it when I learned that this is not a rare occurrence amongst barges and that there were two firms of specialist divers within fifty miles who could undertake the fitting of a new propeller. Did I have a spare? No? Well, that *was* serious. Propellers were specially cast to meet the requirements of each barge; they could not be obtained from stock.

I descended into the bilges to see whether there might perhaps be a spare there. There were three: the first had only two of its three blades, the second only three out of four and the third was immense, at least twice as large as required. I telephoned again and arranged for a search to be made in Antwerp, one of the homes of my type of propeller. As the engine had not been able to develop its full number of revolutions with the existing screw, I wanted one with a slightly reduced pitch. Meanwhile there was nothing to do but wait.

We were moored in a very pleasant position and decided to make the best use of the opportunity to undertake a little maintenance. Out came the paint brushes, the scrubbing brushes, the varnish brushes and assorted tins of this and that and within a short time we had taken on the appearance of any other bargees.

Indeed we could happily have spent several weeks in this area, time permitting, exploring the French Ardennes. Apart from two canal cuts which lop off long loops, one follows the river as it meanders round hills and villages. Often one passes them on three sides and the effect is disconcerting. The best-known hills are the Roches aux Sept Villages, Roches de Laifour and Les Dames de Meuse. The Ardennes provide superb walking country and are particularly beautiful in spring. At Monthermé, the Meuse is joined by the Semoy river which rises far away toward Luxembourg. It is beautiful all the way and can provide another excellent canal voyage. Between Revin and Mézières there is an intermittent passenger service on the Meuse.

After two days a propeller of exactly the right size was located in Antwerp and the following day it arrived, complete with mechanic and frogman. Theirs was not a job I

'L'homme grenouille'
at work on the
broken propeller

envied. The mechanic stood knee deep in sump oil at the
far end of the engine-room bilge and tried to disconnect
the propeller-shaft. Had we a propeller-shaft key? Had we?
I had no idea, but on the whole I suspected that we had not.
Had we a spare thingumajig? I could not be certain. Surely
we had a right-angled left-handed spanner? I very much
doubted it. The mechanic was clearly appalled by the dis-
organised state of our engine-room equipment and kept returning to his car to contrive makeshift tools, each time
leaving a trail of oil and sludge behind him on the deck
that had just received its first proper clean.

L'homme grenouille, however, had an even less joyous
task. It was not a warm day but immediately upon arrival,
with a remarkable lack of inhibition, he took off every stitch
of clothing and donned a rubber suit. He then suspended
from the stern rail a basket containing an assortment of
tools and lowered it into the water. Two large yellow air
cylinders were harnessed onto his back, and these connected
to a face-mask.

I fixed a ladder to the side of the barge to facilitate his
entry and he positioned himself at the top of the ladder
facing in toward the deck. I had supposed that he was about
to descend the ladder placed there for the purpose, but the
presence of one or two onlookers must have provoked him
into showing off a little expertise. For, with a preparatory
flexing of the muscles as the only warning, he jumped high
into the air, performed a neat backward somersault and
plummeted into the obscure depths of the Meuse. Several
minutes later a hammering sound came from the region of
the propeller and this persisted almost continuously for
over an hour, ceasing only momentarily when the frogman
broke surface to communicate with the mechanic. Eventually a cable was lowered and tied round the broken screw,
which was then removed from its shaft and heaved to the
bank for inspection. We asked what it had fouled and were

ı

told waterlogged driftwood. How did they know it was drift-wood and not a stone, for example? Ah, the mechanic ex-plained, it was easy to tell; for if it was caused by wood, it broke in the way we saw; if on the other hand it was caused by a stone, then it broke like this—and he described with his finger a line across the blade exactly where the break already was.

The new propeller was an instant success. Our speed increased yet further and for the first time we had some worthwhile stopping power. We made very pleasing pro-gress through the next twenty miles of the Ardennes and it seemed that after all the mechanical vicissitudes we had suffered, we were in for a run of luck. We had just reached the famous reach of the Meuse near Monthermé when I became aware that our ship was starting to vibrate again in a curious manner. With the sick feeling that forecasts serious mechanical troubles, I descended into the engine-room. I did not have far to look. Water was spraying in-wards through the propeller-shaft bearing. So that was it! The broken propeller had caused wear on the bearing and now it had collapsed.

I took the advice of a passing bargee and continued very slowly to Charleville. Although we felt dejected at the time, the situation was not in fact too desperate. We were due to return to England in two days in any case.

Gradually the Ardennes hills flattened out and became less afforested and soon the suburbs of Charleville came in sight. We had been told that we should find in Charleville a man who specialised in just our sort of problem. Arriving at the town centre, we passed a barge loading coal and con-sulted with the Dutch bargee. He knew the representative's telephone number and said that we could telephone from the nearby Café du Port.

I entered and asked *Madame* for the number. I wondered why she stared so at the piece of paper on which I had written it.

'You wish to speak to M'sieur Lareine?'

'Yes,' I replied. 'You recognise his telephone number?'

'M'sieur Lareine, there is someone who wishes to speak to you,' and she introduced me to the man standing next to me at the bar. At once there was general interest. Something unusual had happened. Everyone gathered round to hear what was afoot.

As the sad mechanical tale unfolded itself, there were expressions of sympathy from all the bargees present. Everyone bought wine, and still more wine. Then they all came in a body to see the *Virginia Anne*. I shook at least a dozen hands and acknowledged any number of expressions of goodwill as one by one they took themselves back to the café.

With a minimum of formality I handed over to the man answering to the name I had been given the keys of the *Virginia Anne* and extracted a promise that all would be ready by the time I returned. That this man was not entirely genuine I did not at the time remotely suspect.

13

A sudden list to starboard

'To think that this time tomorrow we shall be sailing south again.' We were packing the car one evening in August in readiness for an early start the next day. 'I suppose everything will be ready,' I added, slightly uneasy at the total absence of correspondence from the man into whose hands the *Virginia Anne* had been placed. 'Oh surely,' my wife comforted. 'He said the repairs would be finished by the end of June. Besides, he promised he wouldn't let us down with *"la parole d'un Ardennais"*.' Reassured, I continued my efforts to stuff fifty cubic feet of luggage into thirty cubic feet of space. We were taking for the first time our two eldest children, Hugo aged seven and Laura, five, and their excitement was intense. Laura had first packed her 'things' in February and had been unpacking and repacking ever since.

The next day it rained continuously. Across north-east France the wet road reflected the interminable avenues of dripping trees, like endless columns of troops doomed in this vast battlefield of Picardy. The battered poppies hung their heads dismally and the lowering skies robbed even the ice-blue chicory of its colour. Splashing cars; deserted villages. Then a break in the cloud and the Meuse valley spread beyond.

A silence charged with excitement accompanied our arrival at the quay in the late afternoon. How soon would we be under way again—one hour, two hours? We hurried over a gang-plank, across an intervening barge and jumped down to the deck of the *Virginia Anne*. I made straight for the engine-room. I could hardly believe it. Nothing had been done; not a thing!

For some minutes I wrestled with an instinctive wish to go at once to the man's house and set about him with a heavy instrument, but it was soon apparent that only a highly constructive plan could now save our voyage from ruin. At the Café du Port I invested a few francs in a *coup de rouge* for the *patron* and some of his *batelier* customers. Two facts emerged. One was that Monsieur Lareine was a man of consummate idleness and the other that there was no other barge-repairing business within a hundred mile radius except one diminutive yard some ten miles away, now alleged to have fallen on evil days. To have the barge towed ten miles was a possibility; a hundred was out of the question.

We set off at once to examine the possibilities of the other yard. Although by this time we had seen quite a number of barge yards, many of them not very large, we had not before come across one which we were able to walk across without even noticing it. Originally this yard had had a slipway with three carriages which could be placed under a floating barge and then winched up on rails to dry land. But the centre carriage and railway had collapsed. To have withdrawn a barge from the water on the two end carriages alone would have been to risk breaking its back. The whole yard was deep in weeds and undergrowth and only the two winches stood above the greenery. No sign of activity disturbed the peace, nor did we think it ever would again. We returned to Charleville in a highly determined state of mind and with a singleness of purpose that was soon to become all too apparent to the proprietor of the miserable, debilitated business that now jeopardised our holiday.

Learning a language, like falling in love perhaps, is a progressive process and it is difficult, if not impossible, to look back and say that at one particular hour or day one passed the point of no return, the moment when everything dropped into place. But, in retrospect, if ever such a moment did exist in the long, painful process of familiarising myself with the perplexities of the Gallic tongue, I can place it as having occurred that very evening. Having with some guile lured my enemy into the saloon of the *Virginia Anne* and plied him with a good measure of whisky, I was startled to hear myself treat this braggart to an incensed harangue. Excuses were dismissed with further accusations, insults with curses. Arms flew through the air in eloquent support of their owners' arguments, though no blows were actually struck. Having long been an admirer of such emotional outbursts amongst the French, I had now actually participated. I felt I had arrived.

But it was not a reassuring meeting for all that. The truth had finally emerged. Never before had Monsieur Lareine undertaken this operation; indeed he had never even raised a barge from the water. He had the necessary equipment, which he had made himself, but he had doubts as to its efficacy. The 'necessary equipment' consisted of two huge tanks placed side by side, separated by a distance of seven or eight feet and connected to each other by inter-communicating pipes. One of the two tanks supported an eight-foot tower. The entire assembly was known as the *cuve*. It was a standing joke amongst the local bargees as it had been incorrectly made.

In principle, the tanks were filled with water and sunk the necessary distance (the tower still protruding above the water level) so that the stern of the barge would float on the top. The water was then pumped out through a hose lowered through the tower and the stern of the barge would then rise with the tanks. In order to ensure that the *cuve* sank evenly it was necessary to have separate control valves to each tank, but this requirement had been neglected. More sinister still, I now discovered the reason for the scoundrel's doubts. He had in fact attempted to undertake the operation somewhat half-heartedly the week before and in sinking the *cuve*, one tank had filled quicker than the other and the whole apparatus had reared up on end, nearly crushing him against the side of the next barge. This had alarmed him sufficiently to make him unwilling to try again. Excuses were not lacking. He had to go to Paris on urgent business and there was nothing more to be said. If I wanted to undertake the work using his workmen, all well and good. I agreed and on the back of a writing pad he wrote out a note to his two workmen advising them of this arrangement. Monsieur Lareine left for 'Paris'.

The next day the two workmen began the task of sinking the *cuve*. They were not enthusiastic about the prospects of success. And indeed, almost at once it started to list dangerously. The quayside intelligence grapevine is one of the most prolific and we did not have to wait long for spectators to arrive. I had reserved for myself the task of directing operations and I had no sooner started to cajole the two men with a mixture of advice and exhortation than I found myself competing with several others whose advice did not begin to agree with mine. Some of the advisers became participants, so eager were they to prove the soundness of their own theories. Unfortunately much of their labour was to no avail as the efforts of one were in direct opposition to those of another. Soon the top surface of the *cuve* was covered in operatives despite a threatening list. Cables secured each corner to bollards and davits on the two barges alongside us. These cables had failed to prevent the *cuve* from plunging on one side and now as I watched I could see that one of the cables was under intolerable strain and was protesting in a rising chromatic scale of warning clicks. Suddenly the davit to which it was attached could stand the strain no longer; its tubular support was wrenched from its mounting and it hung drunkenly over the side of the adjacent barge. Immediately the *cuve* toppled over, sending its crew scrambling for access to one or other of the surrounding barges.

It took all of five minutes for everyone to stop talking at once. One or two of the volunteers had received a nasty shock and it was not long before they noticed that it was time for lunch. The two workmen now required considerable reassurance before they could be persuaded to return to the apparatus. Understandably, for as they descended the ladder, it suddenly heaved like a surfacing whale and settled on its side. A mild panic ensued; the onlookers jostled each other along the narrow gangways to avoid being within range of a snapping hawser; mutual accusation flew from one barge to the other. Gradually this resolved itself into a comprehensive indictment of the absent Monsieur Lareine. A distant factory hooter announced the official lunch hour and in less than two minutes I was on my own, left to reflect upon the forlorn prospect with which I was faced.

It took a day and a half and great reserves of anger and patience to submerge the *cuve*. At the very moment when it had finally been coaxed into a reasonable position on the bed of the river, Monsieur Lareine returned from 'Paris' expecting acclamation for the success of his service. He was received in stony silence as he climbed down onto the projecting tower. Meanwhile my wife, busy slooshing buckets of water over the scrubbed deck and unaware of Monsieur Lareine's presence on the tower, just below the stern of the

Heavy list to starboard at Charleville-Mézières

Virginia Anne, shot her last bucket of water between the deck and the stern rail where it hit Monsieur Lareine squarely in the back. A wild snort of rage and the beginning of a torrent of abuse were cut short by the applause that this incident provoked.

The *Virginia Anne* was floated slowly back until the wheel-house was above the *cuve* and then secured to the sandwiching barges. A hose was lowered in through the tower and attached to an ancient motor-pump. Two frustrating hours later the engine of the pump had been started; one hour later still the pump had been successfully primed and the evacuation of the water from the *cuve* got under way. By slow degrees the stern rose from the water and a blade of the propeller surfaced, followed by a second and finally by the propeller boss itself. The pump was stopped and Monsieur Lareine allowed himself the flicker of a sneer. Fate was not slow to react. A sudden tautening of a securing cable and then, imperceptibly at first but gaining speed gradually, the *cuve* started to settle toward one side. The *Virginia Anne* followed.

For the second time during my captaincy I had to order 'Abandon Ship', this time from the safety of an adjacent barge where I was standing at the time. Somehow the dramatic content of the command is largely lost if the captain has already fled. Soon after my wife and children had reached safety, the *Virginia Anne* lurched to starboard and stopped with a twenty degree list. Monsieur Lareine looked suitably humiliated. The background of abusive commentary soon reasserted itself.

We spun a web of ropes, hawsers and chains to prevent a further list. Darkness fell and, tired out from nervous strain, we fell asleep in our tilting beds.

The following day we were again at the mercy of this charlatan mechanic whose technical incompetence was equalled only by the inadequacy of his workshop. Tempers were short from the start. I had not slept well at such a steep incline and Monsieur Lareine, having overslept, arrived late. The first task was to remove the propeller from the shaft, and this he attempted to achieve without getting his hands dirty. Progress was slow and I was soon infuriated.

Eventually the propeller was removed and it only remained to withdraw the propeller shaft. A monstrous difficulty now arose. Owing to the increased length of the new engine, the shaft could not be withdrawn without the entire engine being taken out. It seemed that we were doomed to stay here for ever.

In a last desperate effort to reverse the trend of events, I hurried off to the workshop at the other side of the town. I found two mechanics making a desultory attempt to mend a motorcycle. They reacted at once to an impassioned appeal, returned with me to the boat and set about removing the engine. Responding to what is known as a consideration, they agreed to work through the night.

There was nothing I could do until the shaft had been replaced. I sat down in the wheel-house and, for the first time since arriving, looked about me. Across the river, the tall ramparts of the ancient citadel of Mézières rose sheer from the water. Two huge, featureless blocks of flats replaced the old war-gutted buildings. A continuous buzz of traffic came from the direction of the bridge a few hundred yards upstream connecting Charleville with Mézières. The sudden thunder of a train crossing the iron bridge just downstream, the occasional hoot of an approaching barge and the intermittent hammering from a boat moored behind us gave perspective to Henri's quieter but rhythmic spitting.

Henri and his barge form part of the permanent scenery

171

of the port. His is one of the last two engineless barges in the district. The *Compagnie Générale de Traction des Voies Navigables*, known as the CGTVN, used to maintain a diesel tractor for the towing of Henri and his boat, but since his partner died two years ago, Henri has not moved from his mooring. In faded blue patchwork denims, Henri sits on a bollard on his deck, chewing tobacco and spitting with great accuracy at little knots of rubbish floating slowly by. After an hour or more of bollard-sitting he will carefully rise, rag in hand, and start cleaning some small part of his already immaculate boat, victim to a habit imposed by three score years of barge-living. Occasionally he indulges in the pleasure of repainting some piece of equipment. That particular day he had just completed the painting of the windlass, each spoke a different colour. Toward evening he descends the spiral staircase with its polished brass rail to his galley and a few minutes later a thin column of pale blue wood smoke appears from the stove-pipe chimney, heralding the succulent aroma of his *pot-au-feu*. The spiral staircase is panelled in a falsely painted *trompe l'oeil*, which gives a curious effect. Two small alcoves in the staircase wall contain a horse and a dying gladiator in bronze. Henri slowly emerges again, exchanging slippers for deck shoes, and settles on his bollard to await the boiling of his soup.

A game of *boules* was in progress along the quay outside the Café du Port. Inside the occasional banging of a fruit machine testified to the continuous custom of a hard core of *bateliers* whose daily consumption of *rouge* totals many litres. A huge pike, alleged to have been twenty-two years old, had just died in the glass tank hardly larger than himself and *Madame la Patronne* was not her usual self as a result. The barge on our outside was for sale but was currently being inhabited by two long-haired youths who only returned at night at a suspiciously late hour. The front hold contained six chickens who pecked around in the bilge for grains of corn from the last cargo.

As I looked, Henri got up and with one hand took hold of a long barge pole and lowered it into the water. I looked down and saw a rat swimming vainly away from the pole. Henri pulled it in to the barge and dragged it up the side. With his free hand he picked up a length of iron pipe and banged it on the head, the released rat falling dead into the river. A red splash of blood on the black paintwork marked the scene of the murder.

But after a while I suspected that a visit to the workshop would be wise. The mechanics had probably by now been given other work by Monsieur Lareine. The workshop was situated in the least salubrious part of the town, at the end of a street of slums ironically named *Onze Novembre*. Opposite stood a café, the *Tout Va Bien*. This turned out to be Monsieur Lareine's hideout, the scene of his indolence, and the café's name the expression of his personal philosophy. The work was proceeding, however, and I was assured that by early the next morning the shaft would be ready.

Back at the port we made ready for a possible departure the following day. We ran a hose out to a water point, replenished the tanks and mounted a major shopping expedition into Charleville. There was a market in progress in the *Place Ducale*, a square reminiscent of the similarly arcaded *Place des Vosges* in Paris and the redeeming feature of the town. In a corner of the market was a gypsy selling an assortment of bric-à-brac, including a five-foot high mirror which caught my eye. It was a genuine eighteenth century mirror in excellent condition. The frame was a modern copy but elegant. Thirty-five shillings (or 175p as it is now) secured this bargain and it now lends a classical air to the saloon of the *Virginia Anne*.

The chief object of my search was paraffin. The refrigerator runs on it and my original stock of Dutch paraffin was nearly exhausted. I addressed myself to the nearest hard-

ware and ironmongery shop.

'*Paraffine? Hélas!* We do not have it any more, not since the war.' I vaguely wondered why and headed for the next one.

'*Paraffine, hein? Non, Monsieur, pas ici.* Try at the chemist's round the corner,' the assistant added with a wry smile, the reason for which became apparent just as I asked the chemist for this commodity. Dim but unpleasant memories of childhood health purges came back to me and while the good man disappeared to find a bottle of this depressing corrective, I fled the shop.

'*Paraffine?*' repeated the man in a fuel wholesalers to which a policeman had directed me. 'What do you want with *paraffine,*' he asked in genuine astonishment. 'It must be thirty years since anyone asked for that.' I was getting desperate. 'Never mind,' I said, 'just tell me where I can buy it in Charleville and I shall be much obliged.'

'There's just one possibility,' he said after prolonged thought. 'An ironmongery and joinery shop at the other side of the town; it is just possible you might get it there.' I dragged myself on to the shop with my still empty jerry-can.

'*Paraffine? Eh bien!* Perhaps there is still some. I will ask the *patron.*' He returned with a ladder which he leaned against a tall range of shelves, climbed to the top and I lost him amongst the hanging frame saws and spirit levels. The shop smelt deliciously of turpentine and tar. After much rummaging around, the assistant returned with a dusty brown paper package. '*La paraffine!*' he announced triumphantly, banging the package down on the counter. I undid it out of curiosity. Paraffin-wax! Tallow! So that is what I had spent the afternoon running to earth! 'But it is paraffin oil I want,' I explained in a flat voice, pouring the few remaining drops from the jerrycan onto my fingers. He smelt it.

'*Ah! Vous voulez du pétrole?* Whyever didn't you say so?'
It would be interesting to know how many Frenchmen in England blow themselves up each year due to this linguistic trap.

It had been our intention to start out as soon as possible the following day. We breakfasted early and then stepped ashore to say goodbye to the *patron* and *patronne* of the Café du Port. Early as it was, it was unfortunately not too early to drink a toast to the voyage. The sound of the cork being removed must have reached the peculiarly sensitive hearing of the nearby *bateliers* for within minutes all our friends and acquaintances of the last two days appeared. Everyone joined in the well-wishing and as one round of *rouge* led to the next, the scene took on the appearance of the finale in a rather poor comic opera.

By the time we were back on board I was in no condition to enter the next lock which was set at right angles to the river and in full view of the small crowd assembled in the happy expectation of seeing the lock demolished. But a further delay at the last minute gave me time to recover. Just as we were casting off I noticed that one of our steel hawsers had been exchanged for a shorter one full of nasty kinks. Steel hawsers are too valuable to abandon, so I decided that it must be looked for at the risk of causing embarrassment. I had only to glance in the direction of Henri's boat to see it neatly coiled on the floor of the forward hold. I drew Henri's attention to it; he simply shrugged his shoulders and spread his hands in a gesture that said as plainly as words that findings are keepings. Whilst I effected the exchange, Henri looked on unperturbed and continued his rhythmic spitting. Then with a final handshake all round we at last pulled away.

After a short distance I went down to the engine-room to make certain that the new transmission was behaving itself, only to find that the room was flooded to a depth of about a foot. It was all I could do not to lose heart completely. The hull must have been distorted by being raised on the *cuve* and the water be pouring in between the plates. I shouted up for the engine to be stopped. During the few minutes that we drifted, the water appeared not to be getting any deeper. We restarted the engine and I noticed then a commotion in the water beneath the engine; a cooling circuit drain tap had been left on. The panic was over.

At last we were under way again, and passing the entrance to the Canal des Ardennes at Pont à Bar.* Soon after, away from the Ardennes to our left, the river Chiers joined the Meuse, offering 98 kilometres of peaceful Class I canoeing.

The sun was shining and the birds were singing happily. A light breeze skimmed across the buttercup-yellow fields. I felt suddenly exhilarated. Gradually I pushed the throttle forward and saw for the first time the full effect of the new propeller. It was magnificent. The *Virginia Anne* surged forward and in less than a mile had overtaken two other barges. For the first time since I purchased her, everything worked and it seemed at last that we were all set to make some real progress. She might well be one of the oldest barges, but she was also one of the fastest.

*See Notes

M

14

'La manivelle! La manivelle!'

I will not attempt to describe the rest of the journey day by day, although in retrospect certain days stand out for their beauty or for their eventfulness. Variety was never lacking. Whether we were crossing wide alluvial plains before ranges of hills, as when we were approaching Dun-sur-Meuse; whether we were confined to narrow valleys or exploring the monuments of man, like the fortress of Sedan: no two days were remotely the same. Fresh scenes and new faces saw to that in any case. And the unexpected is an inseparable part of inland waterway travel.

As we proceeded up the Meuse, the river narrowed and became shallower and in consequence longer sections of canal became necessary. Both the navigable portions of the river and the connecting lock cuts are known collectively as the *Canal de l'Est.**

Perhaps this is the moment to digress briefly on the essential features of the French canal system. Though by far the greatest concentration of waterways is in the north-east corner of France, some of the most interesting are neverthe-

See Notes

*The gates of
Verdun from the
saloon*

less in the centre (Burgundy), the north-west (Brittany) and the south (Midi). With the general exception of the Seine and the Rhône, which can accommodate larger shipping, most of the canals are built to take a standard barge having a length of 38.5 metres (125 feet), a beam of 5.20 metres (17 feet) and a maximum draught of 1.80 metres (6 feet). These dimensions were established by a man called Freycinet and became incorporated in an Act of 1879. Subsequently many of the canals were enlarged to meet these dimensional requirements (which allow for a capacity of 300-350 tons) and it is on account of this relatively generous capacity that the French waterways are still commercially viable.*

I remember a certain spot on the canal just before Verdun. Historic Verdun, that legend unmatched for horror. It claims to be the battlefield with the highest density of dead per square yard throughout recorded history, an unenviable claim, and certainly this whole area of the Meuse valley, despite recent reafforestation, remains indefinably gloomy. Even birds deliberately shun the shelter of the thickets. Rotting boots, gas masks, steel helmets and the impedimenta of infantrymen still litter these deserted places and I know of no countryside more lonely, more steeped in sorrow than here. But amongst so many thousands who died anonymously, one man was granted a temporary reprieve by Verdun in 1916 in order that his name might be recorded by history—General Karl-Heinrich von Stupnagel, German Military Governor in Paris and one of the leading plotters in the unsuccessful bomb attempt on Hitler's life in 1944. Returning to Germany where trial and certain death awaited him, he was travelling, at his own request, by way of Verdun. His guards agreed his request to get out of the car near the position where he had commanded a battalion in 1916. Hearing a shot, his guards ran

See Notes

to find him floating here in the canal. He had succeeded only in putting out his eyes and it was left to the Gestapo to kill him by strangulation and thus claim yet another victim for Verdun.

It was a contrast, after Verdun, to pass through a land of rich water-meadows.

One morning we had weighed anchor at about half past six. It was one of those days when all the world knows it is going to be as hot as can be. The dew was exceptionally heavy and the mist so thick that we had to wait some time for it to clear sufficiently before we could proceed. The water was absolutely still except for the occasional splash of a water rat or moorhen. Rounding a bend, I saw an unforgettable scene from a Chinese print: two fishermen at either end of a punt, silhouetted against a silver mirror of water and a background of mist, completely motionless. On either side the still reeds, their cuneiform leaves rising ladder-like from the water. A little further and the mist lifted to reveal a meadow mauve with autumn crocus; and everywhere the grey-green willows of Corot, the bending rod of the August fishermen piercing their foliage.

Later whole families gathered in compact groups around the straw-hatted, bulky figure of *Monsieur* clutching his rod in silent concentration, his wife knitting distractedly while the children dangled their legs in the water and the dog, gorged with the picnic remnants, lay in the shade exhausted by the heat and by the frustration of staying so long in one place. Like raised swords at a military wedding, the rods rose in succession as we progressed along the river. Languorous cattle, their forelegs in the cool water, stood in motionless groups. Here in the slow summer of provincial France activity is absorbed by somnolence, the new is assimilated by the old and life is lived at the speed the Almighty intended. The church clocks chime with a drowsy restraint. The black-dressed *grand'mère* strolls lingeringly along the

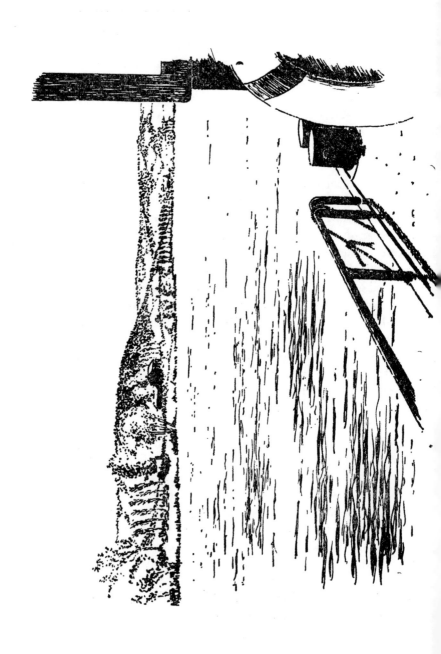

river bank, pausing to pick the most succulent leaves for the family rabbit. Time to stand and stare, time to converse, time to be polite. Complete peace. And flowers everywhere; the banks purple with loosestrife, mallow and willow herb. Old stone walls, ancient mellowed tiles, windows aflame with potted geraniums.

We seemed to be the only things moving. We were the ones who were out of step. I stopped the engine and we drifted slowly to rest against the current. I walked to the bow and, greatly daring (never having ventured it before), released the anchor brake. An almighty clattering, a tremendous splash and the three hundredweight of anchor plunged into the water. It held. We were halted in the midst of this paradise of rural inactivity. It was ninety degrees in the wheel-house and one of the children was despatched to fetch iced beer from the refrigerator; the condensation on the outside of the bottle gave me an almost tangible thrill. We erected on the upper deck a huge sun-umbrella found in the bilges, placed chairs beneath and lowered the bathing ladder over the side. The afternoon was yet young and, relaxing into one of the chairs and sipping the beer, I fell into a contented reverie. Everything was perfect.

The warm smell of the river was a clear invitation to bathe. An agreeable breeze had risen and it sent little ripples lapping against the side of the boat where the children were swimming about on the end of lines. The barge looked immense from water level and I swam a little downstream to view it from further away. I had gone 100 yards or so and was just about to turn when I heard a shout from my wife, 'The boat's adrift!' She was broadside on to the river, obstructing most of the navigable portion. I was just debating whether she was in fact adrift or simply swinging around the anchor when another shout reached me. 'There's a barge coming downstream!' No sooner said than

I heard the deep drone of an approaching barge. It had been so long since we had met any traffic that I had forgotten all about it. It would take me minutes to swim back to the barge; then there were the children to be embarked, the anchor to raise—if indeed we could—the engine to start and the boat to bring round into the stream again. The question seemed to be whether or not the approaching barge would be able to stop in time.

I reached the ladder just as the other barge came round the corner. My frantic waves received a long blast on the ship's horn in reply. It would be on us in less than a minute, for it was unladen and travelling at great speed with the current. 300 yards from us, the skipper moved his engine into full astern, only then appreciating the full extent of our immobility. His boat being unladen, the propeller tunnel was partly above water and, with the sudden change of direction of the water in the tunnel, cascades were forced up behind the boat. It was spectacular but hardly effective and we ourselves were powerless to avert the imminent catastrophe. The skipper for his part abandoned all attempt at stopping and, shutting off his engine, slid into the narrow channel between our bow and the bank. With nothing more than a scraped hull between us to show for it, we were more than ever convinced that the *Virginia Anne* bore a charmed life.

I shouted some feeble apology and prepared to have the dregs of the French language hurled at my head, instead of which the skipper raised a bottle of red wine to his lips and drank our health as he passed, laughing so much that the spilled wine ran down his vest.

The keeper at the next lock attempted to sell us an im-

mense and terrifying-looking carp. It was the very last thing
we wanted and we tried to say so as politely as possible. But
he was determined to sell it at any price and carried on a
one-sided bargaining against himself as he wound the gates
and lowered the paddles.

'*Quinze francs, Monsieur!*'

'*Non merci, Monsieur.*'

'*Alors douze francs, Monsieur.*'

'*Merci, Monsieur.*'

'*Allez! Dix francs, Madame!*' turning his attention to
Madame.

'*Merci, Monsieur.*'

'*Il est beau comme poisson. Un repas entier. Délicieux!
Je vous demande seulement huit francs; c'est pour rien.*'

'*Non merci, Monsieur. Nous n'aimons pas beaucoup
cette espèce de poisson.*'

'*Alors, cinq francs, Madame.*'

Once again we politely declined, but even so we only just
managed to avoid being given it as a present. Doubtless the
lock-keeper liked carp no more than we did.

Although none of the locks in this region appears on the
face of it to have much to do with commerce, there are in
point of fact few that are not engaged in some form of profit-
making activity. The usual commodity is vegetables. They
are set out on a table ready to purchase, though if you see
something in the vegetable garden that takes your fancy you
ask to buy it. Similarly at locks where chickens are kept it
is often possible to buy eggs. The advantage of this system is
that the produce is not only completely fresh but much
cheaper than it would be in a shop. It saves time too.
Poultry, bread, oil and so on are often available, whether on
display or not, and the regular traffic knows exactly what
can be bought and where. The price of course varies from
customer to customer and I was interested to hear, one day
while I was standing painting a canvas at a lock for several

hours, the different prices quoted for the same thing. On this occasion the lock-keeper's wife was especially anxious to sell a large domestic rabbit. As successive barges were being locked through, she carried the unfortunate animal out and quoted prices which varied by some twenty per cent. She finally succeeded in selling it to the smartest-looking barge for the highest price.

———

There was a feeling of considerable achievement when we reached the southernmost limit of the Meuse, or more precisely the junction of the northern branch of the *Canal de l'Est* with the *Canal Marne au Rhin*.

Some 400 miles from its mouth and 70 from its source, the Meuse itself is about the size of the Thames at Oxford; only a few of the last 80 miles or so are navigable, the Canal following a lateral course. Having proceeded thus far in a generally southerly direction, we now turned east along the *Marne au Rhin* canal.* (This is the canal that can be seen periodically from the Paris-Nancy train.) It passes through a chalky region and the particles of chalk held in suspen-sion give the water a curious aquamarine appearance. A light railway with conspicuously unparallel tracks follows the canal along the towpath and from time to time a sad-looking lilliputian diesel engine belonging to the CGTVN stands in a siding. We never actually saw one in use and in theory they are now no longer used.

Our progress along the first section of the canal was un-eventful by our standards. We failed to take one particu-larly sharp bend and struck the bank a glancing blow which broke some glasses in the saloon. Then again we scraped

*See Notes

The Virginia Anne being towed into the Foug tunnel

along the hull of an ancient wooden barge which was rounding a bend on the wrong side and appeared to have nobody aboard at all; it must have been steered from a position other than the wheelhouse, though I wondered which. But by now we were taking events of this kind altogether in our stride.

In due course we came to the tunnel of Foug. At this point the canal passes beneath a high hill for a distance of almost 1,000 yards (867 metres). Passing through under one's own power is forbidden; instead the barges are attached to one of the diesel engines and pulled through in convoy in alternate directions. These tractors have a top speed of nearly one mile per hour but ours was no longer in the peak of condition and I doubt if it made half that speed. Half-way through the tunnel, noticing that the cab of the tractor was loaded with boxes of French beans, we opened negotiations with the driver and by the end of the tunnel we had agreed a fair price. The beans were duly weighed and wrapped. Who, passing over the summit of the hill above our heads, would have suspected such subterranean business transactions?

At the far end of the tunnel we emerged into a basin heading a flight of 14 descending locks in the space of only 6 miles. We had now to drop 150 feet to the level of the Moselle.

The first of these locks consisted of a very fine double pen enabling traffic to be raised and lowered simultaneously, although as all the locks on either side are single pen it would seem to be a completely pointless structure. All the locks in this section are controlled hydraulically by an operator shut away in a glass-sided control box. We missed enormously the friendly exchange of the hand-operated locks. By contrast the modern ones are soulless and uncongenial and in fact the few lock-keepers we did meet were noticeably less friendly. It merely served as further illustration of the way in which relationships shrink as individuals become progressively isolated by automation. But if it helps to lower the cost of canal upkeep and thus to ensure their continuity, then these 'improvements' must be justified.

Just before the junction of the *Marne au Rhin* canal with the southern branch of the *Canal de l'Est**—which is really the canalised Moselle—we reached the city of Toul and tied up in the spacious port. The Moselle at Toul, after its swift descent from the Vosges, flings out a curious elbow and changes direction abruptly. Right up until the Pleistocene era the Moselle turned west at this point and rushed headlong into the Meuse. But subsequently the Moselle was lured east by a tributary of the river Meurthe which had eroded the hillside and gained a lower level. The ancient bed of the Moselle can still be seen to the west of Toul, near Pagny-sur-Meuse.

Toul itself is a beautiful old town largely contained within its ancient defensive walls. The cathedral of St-Etienne is worth a visit in any case, boasting a number of unusual features including a most refreshing absence of stained glass. But it was doubly so that day; the huge organ was being tuned and the clear, pure sound of the solitary notes reverberated around the cathedral with a breathless resonance. The west façade with its two octagonal towers and lanterns is especially striking.

The canal incorporates a section of the town moat on the north side and hugs the towering buttresses. We were rounding one such corner buttress when a bridge, which

*See Notes

must at one time have formed part of the fortifications, loomed up only a hundred yards or so ahead. By this time I had developed an eye for bridge heights give or take the odd inch, and not only did this one look too low and narrow but it also bore a large notice with the words:

DANGER DE MORT
FILS NUS DE HAUTE TENSION

Stopping was out of the question and there was nothing for it but to aim dead centre and hope for the best, as usual. My concern for the bridge, or for the barge for that matter, was as nothing compared to my fixation over the high-tension wires, now all-too-clearly visible. To this day I do not know whether there was no electricity in the wires or whether the wooden roof of the wheel-house insulated us when the inevitable collision occurred.

Tied up to a quay near the entrance to the canal were three very new-looking motor launches flying the German flag. All three were painted in an identical colour scheme, with any unpainted area chromed. Evidently a *Familiegruppe* on holiday. In the saloon of the largest we could see the family sitting around a table laden with food and bottles. *Würst und bier*, we observed, although it was about half past three in the afternoon.

A little way up the Moselle we stopped to examine a barge being constructed in a very primitive shipyard. A 600 ton vessel of surprisingly modern appearance with luxurious skipper's quarters was gradually taking shape in what appeared to be an avenue of chestnut trees. The 'yard' consisted of a depression in the ground lower than the normal height of the river; the water could be shut off by means of a crude sluice and the area pumped dry. It had evidently been empty for a long time, for plant life was flourishing. At one end was a small sawmill and metal workshop no larger than the average garage premises. That an undertaking of this size could give birth to such an

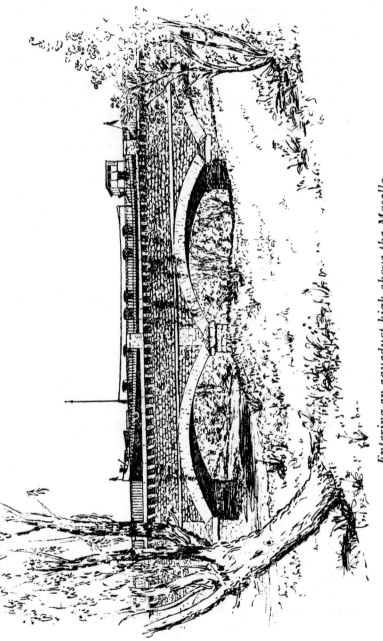

Entering an aqueduct high above the Moselle

immense offspring seemed bizarre.

The river (and lock cuts) is maintained at a more or less constant height by weirs. In effect these are regulated water-falls, the regulation being brought about by variable controls of one sort or another. In this part of the Moselle, the water height is controlled by the number of removable 'needles' inserted edge to edge on the upstream side of permanently positioned horizontal members. The needles are about six foot in length and have the shape of elongated cricket bats. Hundreds are required for each weir. A minia-ture railway, complete with sidings at the terminus near the weir-keeper's house, provides for their transport along the entire length of the weir. The force of water rushing through the weirs is impressive at any time, but with a river in flood the task of removing the needles (sometimes in the middle of the night) is not one that I covet. The sys-tem is a modernised version of that used in very early days on English rivers such as the Thames.

We met an average of only half a dozen barges a day on this canal. Most of them came from Rotterdam and carried coal imported from the United States and loaded into them straight from the cargo vessels. They were bound for the steelworks at Neuves Maisons and the majority were then returning to Holland via the Ruhr with a cargo of Neuves Maisons steel. We were very glad to leave this depressing town behind. As with steel works the world over, the smoke from the furnaces casts a blight over the whole countryside for miles around. The steel traffic turned off down the *em-branchement de Nancy* thus leaving us more or less by our-selves, and indeed we met no further barges for nearly two days. No barges actually in passage that is, for there were a large number of rotting hulks along the edge of the canal. Some were actually lived in, though the profusion of the vegetation sprouting from their sides made it anyone's guess how they remained afloat.

The Flavigny aqueduct, completed in 1893, is a notable piece of engineering by any standards. A little over 400 feet in length, it carries the canal high above the Moselle. It seems altogether remarkable that a stone structure can possibly withstand the weight of water and the buffetings of passing barges. To be sure it does leak toward one end, but not seriously, and the *gardien du pont* assured me that it always had. 'Leave well alone,' he wisely advised in answer to my suggestion that it be mended.

The previous night there had been a storm of fearsome proportions and the *gardien* was glad of the chance to exchange experiences on the subject. He had heard that it had been far worse in southern France. 'Dozens have been drowned', he added vaguely, 'but it does not compare with the time I was visiting my wife's mother in Cannes. It was terrible! Horrifying! The sea actually washed into the casino—yes, the casino!' He was immensely impressed by the extent of the sacrilege and stared at us for full five seconds to make sure that we realised the significance. 'But it was even worse, far worse, when I was in Le Havre one November. The waves were gigantic! Bigger than anything you ever saw,' and he looked desperately around for something higher even than the trees which would do justice to his story. *'Mon Dieu!'* he concluded, reliving his salvation from drowning.

We climbed aboard and the *gardien* sauntered back to his uneventful vegetable garden by way of his fishing rod which he had left resting in a forked stick on the edge of the bank.

N

It might be thought safe to assume that all these weeks of travelling under a variety of conditions had by now inculcated in us the art of passing through locks without incident. But this was not so. Minor incidents were common and were generally caused by an untoward wind catching the bow just as we were entering. But now an entirely new hazard arose.

It was a calm day and we were entering a lock which looked just like any other when I saw the warning notice:
ATTENTION. CETTE ECLUSE LANCE.
It was generally agreed that *lancer* meant 'to throw' and we wondered what the lock could conceivably be throwing. We were soon to discover: it was no lesser object than the barge!

We were secured both fore and aft by a thick nylon rope to the bollards on the lockside. Neither rope was particularly tight, but a friend who was accompanying us stood guard over the forward rope so that it could be tightened as the barge began to move. As the water started to enter the lock the barge drifted slowly backwards and as the ship's bollard came in line with the lock bollard—when the rope was at its shortest—the slack was pulled in. Absolutely nothing happened for about a minute; then suddenly without warning the stern of the barge rose and she was thrown forward toward the front lock gate at alarming speed; the nylon rope snapped with a noise like a pistol shot, cutting the hand of our unfortunate passenger, and the *Virginia Anne* struck the mitre of the lock gates a crashing blow. Although holding back a seven-foot head of water, both gates opened momentarily to admit a cascade of water on to the bow. The impact had knocked us all down and by the time I had picked myself up the doors had banged shut again. The collision had caused the paddle-winding handle to fly high into the air before ricocheting off the deck and plummeting into the lock.

The lock-keeper's wife had been operating the paddles.

'La manivelle! La manivelle!' she kept shrieking, wringing her hands over the loss of the winding handle. *'La manivelle! La manivelle!'* came a chorus of replies from the lock-keeper's house as he, the mother, mother-in-law, grandmother, grandfather, cousins, aunts, uncles and a host of children poured out. On the other side of the lock people seemed to rise out of the ground. Whereas no one but the lock-keeper's wife had witnessed our arrival, now suddenly there were hordes of people all talking at once and all waving their arms.

The loss of the *manivelle* seemed to me to be the least of all the worries. Apart from our wounded passenger, I was concerned about the lock gate itself, to say nothing of the bow of the barge; I felt sure that one or other must have suffered some major damage. But these other matters assumed no importance in the minds of the onlookers, obsessed as they were by the loss of the much-lamented handle. The reason, we learned, was the need to fill in a formidable document rivalling a military accident report, and this was now produced with due solemnity. Moreover, if the handle could not be found we should have to pay a fine. But first there was a possibility that the *manivelle* could be raised from the bottom of the lock by long barge poles fitted with rake-like attachments. Grappling with a 25 foot barge pole in 8 feet of swiftly-flowing water is not unlike trying to stir treacle with a telephone pole. Our attempts proved abortive and there was nothing for it but to complete the form.

The barge was resecured and with the aid of a replacement *manivelle* the water was admitted rather more gently. The close fit of the boat within the lock seemed responsible for the throwing; with only about six inches to spare on either side, the water built up at the forward end of the lock and passed beneath the boat in a great rush, lifting the stern and hurling the vessel forward. Why this had not occurred at previous locks remained a mystery.

N*

As soon as the lock was filled, the process of unwinding the gates began. This was the moment I had been dreading. The bow of the barge was unhurt and that meant that the gate must have taken the shock. The handle turned only half a revolution before it effectively jammed. Immediately the consternation was resumed. The canal would be closed for weeks. The pinion was sheared. Where could a new one be found? How could one possibly tell? What a disaster! The long faces of the crowd were all too eloquent and we felt suitably ashamed. It was not until every facet of the gloomy affair had been aired and argued minutely, some 90 minutes later, that it occurred to the lock-keeper that there might be a spare pinion only two locks away and he set off on his bicycle to look for it. An exhausted lock-keeper returned at length and, after the inevitable round of conflicting advice on the subject of fitting the new pinion, effected the repair. Amidst a great creaking the gates opened and we were waved on, several impatient barges hot on our heels.

'Where does the barge come from anyway?' asked one of the spectators of another.

'From London. That's in Holland, isn't it?'

'Yes, I think so. Ah yes, that's the Dutch flag.'

We let it stand.

15

Gallantry in the coalharbour

If we had disgraced ourselves in the last lock, we were to restore the balance in the next.

In the narrow, deep locks it is customary for the deck-hands to throw up the line with a noose so that the lock-keeper can place it over the bollard. My wife had become adept at it and no longer bothered to watch where the end fell. On this occasion she threw the line up as usual to the passing lock-keeper whose attention was however diverted elsewhere. The noose fell neatly over his head. Feeling the line tighten, my wife started to pull it taut and for a moment, as he teetered toward the edge struggling to free himself, I thought he was going to fall 20 feet onto the barge. But we were cheated of the spectacle of a lifetime as my wife glanced up and released her hold on the protesting lock-keeper.

At about this time we purchased our first copy of the *Journal de la Navigation*, a newspaper circulating only amongst the bargees and devoted entirely to subjects of interest to the *batellerie*. All the births, deaths and marriages are listed, the many accidents discussed in morbid detail and all the items of waterside gossip spread over numerous columns. It also contains much valuable advice about the state of the navigation in various parts and gives up-to-date schedules for the closure of locks for repairs and so on.

The love of gossip amongst the *batellerie* is impressive. As is bound to happen in an isolated, closed society, life-long friendships strengthened by an identity of interests are quickly formed between water-borne families. Acquainted boats passing each other—perhaps unexpectedly and after an interval of years—will invariably stop and spend hours catching up on all the news, regardless of whether or not they are blocking the canal.

South of the *embranchement de Nancy* the canal has only a light traffic and the tow-path is in a very neglected state. Towing by rubber-tyred diesel tractor has recently been suspended since a number of tractors fell into the canal. This has meant the end of motorless barges unless pulled by horse.

As we proceeded south, the bridges became steadily lower and sometimes there was only an inch or two to spare. It seemed only a matter of time before we came to one that would defeat us. Theoretically we should have been able to pass them all, just, but in practice this did not work out. Various factors were to blame. For one thing, if traffic is heavy in a short section of canal, the displaced water pushes up the level appreciably. For another, if the barges are moving in the same direction, the water is shovelled up ahead of them and this too can have a surprisingly significant effect. Indeed, an experienced lock-keeper can tell when a barge is approaching simply by observing the rise of water against the gate. Furthermore, when a lockful of water is released from the section above, the level naturally rises still further and although most canal sections have an overflow for the purpose of regulating the water level—

sometimes the lock gates themselves form the overflow—nevertheless it takes time for the water to escape. Besides all these factors, there is always the possibility that certain bridge structures may have sunk since they were last measured. And then of course the barge itself may draw more or less water according to the amount of bilge water, the contents of the water and fuel tanks and so on. If all the external variables combine against one, it can make a difference of as much as six inches. As a high percentage of the bridges depended in our case on a theoretical clearance of only four or five inches, these considerations were critical.

It was therefore inevitable that sooner or later we should encounter one that left us insufficient space. It now appeared. Trying both sides of the canal made no difference, though after waiting and wondering for about ten minutes the water level did drop just enough for us to ease our way beneath one side of the bridge but not the other. Whilst pondering this situation the water level rose again and we were stuck with the wheel-house neatly caught between the two sides of the bridge. The level never went down again sufficiently for us to escape, so I had to descend to the engine-room and open a valve in the hull. I was soaked in the process of flooding the engine-room with several hundred gallons but it did the trick. A little farther on we not only had to repeat the performance—just as we had pumped the engine-room dry again—but we had also to ask the lock-keeper behind us to let go as much water as he dared.

After the 38th lock up the gradual ascent of the *Canal de l'Est*, the *embranchement d'Epinal* is reached. Immediately after a hideously sharp turning, one encounters the canal bridge over the Moselle. 200 yards long and only a few inches wider than the barge, I defy the most experienced *batelier* to make the crossing without touching the sides. Quite apart from the obvious difficulty of navigation in such confined circumstances, one's attention is distracted by

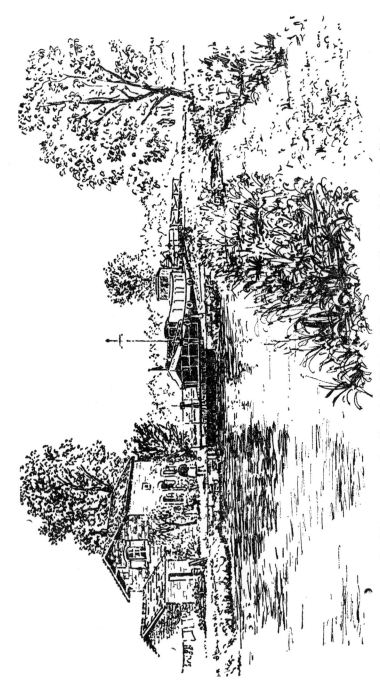

Locking up on the Canal de l'Est, while negotiating for 'chanterelles'

the extraordinary view along the Moselle far below. To cross a river by floating high above it in a ship is for some reason a most curious sensation which has simply to be experienced to be appreciated.

Three kilometres of level canal brought us to the port of Epinal. The approach is through heavily wooded banks, but the beauty is spoilt by the scum on the water, more and more dense toward the town. Being a cul-de-sac, there seems to be an inadequate flow of water to remove it. In the port itself the scum is so thick that one can imagine walking across the surface without fear of sinking. That one in fact cannot was soon to be amply demonstrated. The effect is not improved by the seepage of oil and other matter from the vessels berthed in the port, nor by the thick layer of coal dust from the coal wharfs nor the sprinkling, by way of decoration, of multicoloured litter in various stages of buoyancy.

Depressing as it was, we were obliged to moor here, occupying the remaining berth in the coal wharf. We had planned to leave the barge at Epinal for the winter but now, seeing the conditions, decided to move on if possible. However, we had reckoned without the *Bureau des Ponts et Chaussées*, to whose offices I now bicycled.

'You wish to leave your boat in the canal for the winter, Monsieur?' asked a somewhat surprised official. 'I regret that it is not possible.'

'I realise it is not possible according to the regulations,' I replied, 'but I hope it may be possible to work out some arrangement to the satisfaction of all parties concerned.' He brightened visibly. I had long since discovered that in dealing with French officialdom one should never be depressed by a complete refusal. As often as not it is thrown out as a challenge for a discussion or as a device for indicating that, since it is within their power to prevent you doing whatever it is you want, there may be a consideration involved before a formula can be worked out. But he reinforced his point.

'I am not permitted to allow any vessel to remain unattended without the permission of the regional director at Nancy.'

'Well, would you be kind enough to telephone him for permission?'

'Quite impossible, Monsieur. I am very sorry, but the Director is away. Besides, application has to be made in writing a week before permission is granted. In any case it is unlikely to be granted as there is nowhere suitable for the mooring of a barge in this region.'

'Unfortunately I have to return to England this afternoon, so if you will be good enough to indicate the least inconvenient place for me to leave the barge, I will take it there at once.'

'It is not in any case permitted to leave the vessel without appointing a caretaker. They are not easy to find. Have you anyone in mind?'

I suddenly saw the point of the discussion.

'Well,' I began tentatively, 'I was wondering whether perhaps *you* would consider . . .'

He cut me short.

'If you come back in two hours, perhaps it may have been possible to come to some arrangement. But you understand it will not be easy?'

I thanked him profusely for his sympathetic understanding of my predicament.

A great commotion was in progress back at the barge. Hugo, it seemed, had become bored with wandering along the quay and had devised a game throwing lumps of coal into the port. The effort of throwing one particularly large lump made him topple in after it. Practising his newly acquired art of swimming and trying desperately to see over the top of the floating debris toward some means of escape, he filled the air with cries for help. My wife was below and heard nothing. However the incident had been observed by a passing lorry driver and by a bargee on the opposite side of the port. Both came running round, to be joined soon by others. All lined the edge and shouted. To a man they removed their coats. Not one of them went in. Eventually Hugo managed to grab hold of the anchor which fortunately, but most incorrectly, was at water level since I had not had the energy to finish raising it after its last use.

The noise finally prompted my wife to come up and investigate. The appearance of a woman on the scene encouraged the rescuers to gallantry and two of them went through elaborate preparatory diving motions without actually making the plunge. The third went for more help. It was left to the fourth to board the barge, climb down the anchor chain and effect the rescue. Hugo was covered in black oil and filth and was quickly topped up with neat whisky. He soon recovered from the ordeal without any subsequent ill-effects.

In due course I returned to the office of the *Ponts et Chaussées* and found that everything had been arranged. I was directed to move the barge up toward the summit of the canal where at a particular lock my official would meet me and show me the mooring. Some two hours later this had been achieved.

'You see,' he explained, 'the house just beyond the barge. It is mine. Now we must arrange for a caretaker who can keep it under constant supervision.'

'Yes, of course,' I said with a wink and he ushered me into the house to meet his family.

Within minutes a formal handshaking had put the seal on 'an arrangement to the satisfaction of all parties'.

Epinal is built on both banks of the winding Moselle and extends to a small island formed by the elimination of one of the river's more extravagant curves by a matter-of-fact stretch of canal.

We completed the formalities as rapidly as possible so that we might visit the *Musée international de l'imagerie* on the island and see the prints to which the town gave its name and owed its considerable reputation before the advent of today's flourishing cotton industry. Housed in an old hospital, the collection presents a fascinating history of engraving from its wood-block origins to the present day. Valuable blocks from the early days of the famous *images d'Epinal* in the eighteenth century are supplemented by rare treasures from the other printing centres of France: Toulouse, Chartres, Orléans, Rouen and so on—marvellously expressive work dating back two centuries. Other European countries, Britain included, are also well represented.

As we descended the gangplank with our suitcases, we were hailed from a barge which had just entered the adjacent lock.

'How's the new engine?' asked the skipper, 'And is the propeller behaving itself now? Good luck till we meet again *un de ces jours,*' he called as his descending head disappeared beneath the level of the quay.

We could not recall ever having met him or his barge before but, as we had constantly found, a *batelier* has an astonishing capacity to imbibe every detail of waterway news. He turns it over in his mind and pieces it together during the long, solitary hours and as a rule his memory can be relied upon utterly. And if we had been to the manner born, we should have called back, 'The children, have they recovered from chicken-pox yet? And by the way, don't miss the peas at Lock 28. They're *à point* this week.'

P

16

A veritable catastrophe

I had come out to 'winterise' the boat and make sure that nothing would be damaged by the severity of the Vosges winter. But my arrival had been anticipated by the weather and already several pipes had burst in an exceptionally premature freeze-up. Navigation had been forced to a standstill. My poor boat was freezing inside and out.

It is quite an experience to spend a night in a ship which has been frozen in. A total absence of motion, or sound of ripples lapping against the hull, makes for an eerie stillness; combined with the piercing cold, it gives a tomb-like impression. Then suddenly a crack like a rifle shot bursts in this unnatural calm, followed by a succession of ringing echoes; a shiver runs through the hull and the frozen mooring ropes groan. Then the same exaggerated stillness.

The first night made me think that the hull was being crushed and I ran frantically around the barge smashing the ice with a heavy pole. With the thermometer showing some twenty-five degrees of frost, it took all too little time for the ice to reform and there was little question of sleep.

f the hull is allowed to become surrounded by ice several
nches thick, the steel plates buckle under the tremendous
orces of expansion that the ice creates and the vessel found-
rs. In a cold spell the ice thickens remarkably quickly.
)nly a few days later, when the ice had formed to a thick-
tess of nearly ten inches, a two-ton car skidded and fell over
 bridge onto the canal a short distance from the boat. The
ce remained intact.

I have dwelt on some of the pleasures of barge life in gen-
ral but, should any reader be tempted to contemplate
oining the *batellerie*, I would suggest a few days during a
vinter month on one of the higher waterways.

After several days a sudden thaw encouraged the trapped
bargees to bully the *Service des Ponts et Chaussées* into
breaking the ice. At length the 'ice-breaker' arrived. A
heavy steel pontoon laden with ballast is drawn at high
peed by a powerful tractor on the tow-path. The pontoon
ides up onto the ice and smashes it into large slabs through
vhich the rudder is steered by two men leaning on a long
iller arm and directed by a third who stands in the bow.
This device produces a sensational impact in terms of noise.
ts use is however limited to ice of less than six inches thick-
iess and it may require several passes to produce an adequately free lane for the barges.

Shortly after this operation, I was standing vacantly won-
lering how I could participate in the ice-breaking and
hinking it the most exhilarating sport after the St Moritz
)ob-run, when the first of the trapped barges came inching
ts way through. It was growing dark and the barge moored
 little ahead of me. The skipper suggested opening a bottle
nd I hastened to join him. There, in the curtained wheel-
louse, I saw again the evidence of the stamina required
o pursue this life. The skipper had been up much of the
previous night repairing a pipe in the engine-room that had
rozen and burst. Following in the wake of the ice-breaker,

he had spent most of the day wielding a heavy barge-pole to remove the slabs of ice which jammed his slow path; in the locks especially, every piece of ice had had to be eliminated if the gates were to open and room be made for the barge. His wife for her part had spent the day steering the boat, in between time (one wonders when) doing the laundry and the cooking and looking after the two young children. All day she had been suffering from a raging toothache and her face was swollen painfully; she had been unable to leave the boat to find a dentist without delaying still further their already tardy progress. The four days they spent trapped in the ice had already put paid to the meagre profit they had been hoping to realise on this contract. They had bought their barge on a mortgage and were trying to pay off the instalments without default. To do this, neither husband nor wife could afford to be ill. But none of their cares was allowed to dim their hospitality.

———

I felt apprehension at the thought of leaving the barge unattended throughout the winter. Although the lock-keeper had promised to try to smash the ice around the hull daily, I somehow felt that he would soon tire of this arduous task. Back in England, my worries receded as time and distance separated me from the source of my concern.

———

The winter drew on and I received monthly reports from the lock-keeper's wife confirming that all was well. So it was not until this rhythmic correspondence was interrupted by n unscheduled letter that my anxiety returned.

Panicky handwriting covered a dozen sheets. My immediate return was requested to deal with a triple *désastre*.
Try as I might to mistranslate, the meaning of the word,
whether in French or English, was painfully clear and my
heart sank as I read on.

I learned that a prisoner had escaped from gaol and
found the barge a convenient place into which to break for
shelter. Once inside, it seemed that he had filled himself
up with a bottle and a half of whisky and embarked on a
systematic wrecking of the contents of the boat. To allay
the pangs of hunger, he had taken a tin of *canneloni* and
placed it on the pressure stove; *mais malheureusement*,
instead of paraffin he had filled the stove with petrol and
produced a sizeable explosion. Fire had taken hold and
from carpet to ceiling all was burned and the *canneloni*
arranged around the four walls. No doubt injured and
desperate, this *voyou* had then felt free to arm himself with
a generous supply of clothing, blankets and assorted kit
before fleeing.

I felt sick at the thought of the damage this wretch must
have done. But this was only the beginning, for apparently
it was only the first of three disasters. I read on with mounting anxiety.

The day after the explosion while the *agent* was investi-
gating the crime, a terrible wind had arisen and the barge
had broken its moorings and drifted across towards the far
side of the port where she remained grounded in soft mud
some distance from the bank. The *agent* stranded, they
were unable to pull her back, which event had given rise
not only to the resentment of the *agent* but also to the third
element of the disaster, *une catastrophe véritable!* Did I
remember the details of the mooring? Then perhaps I
could imagine the nature of the event. Indeed I remembered all too well agreeing with the lock-keeper that as

an extra precaution we would tie a rope round the base of the sentry-box-like hut that the French find such an economical solution to the problem of sanitary plumbing. *Hélas*, the distressed woman went on, the rope had failed to break under the tension and the uprooted *cabinet* had plunged into the canal. *Grâce au bon Dieu*, it had been unoccupied at the time. Nevertheless they were all greatly inconvenienced.

The following day I was relieved to receive a further letter saying that a small army of men had succeeded in drawing the *Virginia Anne* back to her rightful berth, in landing the *agent* and in extracting the *cabinet* and restoring it to its former eminence.

In view of this shameful incident, I was all the more surprised to learn, a short while later, that the *Virginia Anne* had finally been accorded the seal of official approval, for she was chosen as the setting for the annual photograph of the brigade of *sapeurs-pompiers* of Epinal, which shows the members lining her deck.

*

The winter passed without further untoward event. I was now a year since our first voyage and I was already looking back over our gradual ascent of the Continental land mass with increasing nostalgia and longing for the next journey.

It might reasonably be felt that all the disappointments and near-disasters of the first year would make one regard the next journey with something other than longing. But if the difficulties make more colourful telling, they are more than compensated for by the joy of realising an ambition. Besides, the passage of time has proved that it is the pleasures that remain fresh in the mind when less happy events have mercifully dimmed. The fact is that in the space of one year I had become a dedicated bargee to whom every mile of canal, every hour of each day, held a fresh enchantment. I felt a kinship for the boat that I could never have believed myself capable of forming; each part had its own identity, a special character that extended almost to the individual rivets. The texture of the wood, the feel of the tarred sides, the smell of the engine-room, the creaking of a straining rope—all these had become an indispensable part of my life. To most people a barge is just a barge and a canal no more than a canal. But to me it is all symbolic of another life.

Poised on the Continental watershed, between north and south, we planned to make a descent of the Vosges and the river Saône, then to go down the fearsome Rhône and across the south of France via the *Canal du Midi* to Bordeaux on the Atlantic coast. The south, the heat and the magic of the Mediterranean. This would take us through some of the most beautiful country in all France. But this all belongs to another story . . .

Notes

General Note

No information has been given on the minimum dimensions of the Dutch waterway locks, since in all cases they are not less than the French minimum dimensions. However, this applies only in respect of those waterways mentioned in this narrative. Since alteration and construction are constantly in progress and since regulations and signals are frequently changing, application should be made to the National Tourist Offices of the country concerned before setting out. This is much to be recommended in preference to the purchase of out-of-date waterway guides and maps, of which there are many. The factual information given in these notes is intended as a general guide only. Local enquiry of those who use the waterways for a living is recommended where possible.

Nonetheless I recommend the purchase of the following guides:

Guide de la Navigation Intérieure. Editions Berger-Levrault, 5, Rue Auguste-Comte, Paris VI. (Vol II contains a generally accurate map of the navigable waterways throughout France. It is more or less indispensable. Vol I contains critical dimensions of the various waterways—not

always accurate—and a great deal of other information which is not essential to the amateur.)
Code de la Route Fluvial. 6th edition (1970). H. Vagnon, 25, Rue Mistral, 69 Caluire.

In addition, the *Journal de la Navigation*, 29, Boulevard Henri IV, Paris IV ème—is able to supply numerous other works on the subject, from the tying of suitable knots to individual river maps. The list (and the cost) changes and therefore application should be made direct. It should however be noted that all these works are in French only.

Particulars of the formalities and documentation required can be obtained from: The Touring Club of France, Avenue de la Grande Armée, Paris (or from the TCF office in London).

Other national tourist offices capable of giving waterway information are: Netherlands: ANWB, 5, Museum-plein, Amsterdam; Belgium: Commisariat Général au Tourisme, Gare Centrale, 1000 Brussels.

Page 98

The Zuidwillemsvaart Canal is partly in Holland and partly in Belgium. The Belgian part is 43 kilometres in length, with 2 locks of 50 metres x 7 metres. The depth is sufficient for a draught of 2 metres 10 cms and there is a minimum bridge height of 4 metres 55 cms. There are 17 locks in the Dutch section, which is 76 kilometres in length.

Page 108

The Albert Canal is 130 kilometres in length, between Liège and Antwerp, and it is equipped with a highly efficient system of locks, 7 in number, so that it is possible to navigate the entire length of the canal in some 12 hours. The dimensions of lock chambers are 136 metres x 13 metres minimum. The depth is maintained at 2 metres 80 cms and the lowest bridge height is 5 metres 25 cms.

Page 110

The Meuse is 656 kilometres in length from source to sea.

It is navigable by canoe (Class I) from Domremy-la-Pucelle (birthplace of Joan of Arc) over a distance of 566 kilometres. In France the canalised length is 252 kilometres, with 59 locks, the smallest of which measure 38.5 metres x 5.20 metres. The river is canalised in Belgium for its course of 126 kilometres, with 18 locks, the smallest of which measure 56 metres x 9 metres. Beyond the Belgian-Dutch border, the river acts as the frontier for 63 kilometres, but the Juliana Canal—wholly within Holland—provides a short cut. From the frontier to the sea, there are 9 locks (all to 2,000 ton standards, including those of the Juliana Canal). From the sea to the junction with the Canal Marne au Rhin, there is a total rise of some 250 metres.

Page 111

The Ourthe river is navigable for 106 kilometres, but the maximum dimensions that can pass the 8 locks are 20 metres length, 3 metres beam and 1 metre draught. Local knowledge is recommended for the passage of this river.

Page 132

The Sambre river and canal is to Freycinet dimensions (see p. 180).

Page 177

The Canal des Ardennes is to Freycinet standards (see p. 180).

Page 178

The Canal de l'Est (Northern Section) extends as far south as the junction with the Canal Marne au Rhin. From the Belgian border at Givet, the length is 272 kilometres, there are 4 tunnels (no facilities for towing) and 59 locks. Due to lack of traffic, it is not well maintained, by French standards, and the depth of the river sections is unreliable.

Page 180

However, the actual size of the different canals does, in practice, vary slightly, particularly as regards headroom and depth. I must warn any reader who has in mind to obtain a boat or barge for use on the Continent to note carefully that—whatever he may have read elsewhere—he may be in trouble if the dimensions of his vessel exceed 38 metres

overall, 5 metres beam or 1.50 metres draught. Again, the
theoretical headroom is 3.70 metres, but in reality for many
canals it is 3.40 metres and for a few tunnels and bridges
(though not on the waterways described in this volume) it
should be possible to reduce the height above water level in
an emergency to 2.50 metres. For the Canal du Midi and
the Canal du Nivernais a maximum length of only 30
metres is possible, and for the canals of Brittany only 25
metres (with a beam reduced to 4.50 metres for the latter).
This excepts the Vilaine in Brittany and certain other
minor waterways where dimensional restrictions are more
severe.

The Canal de l'Est, like all others in France at the present time, is entirely free to foreigners. Our canal dues for
the entire voyage through Holland, Belgium and France
were 5½p.

Page 186

The Marne au Rhin canal links up the Paris and Northern regions of France with the east and Germany. There
are 160 locks, 5 tunnels and the Saint Louis-Arzviller in-
clined plane over a length of 313 kilometres, but no unusual dimensional restrictions. Although only the tunnel
of Foug is encountered in this narrative, it should be noted
by intending travellers that, with the exception of the tunnel at Liverdun, towing is obligatory. In principle the
timings are:

    Tunnel at Mauvages:
    Toward the east: 06.00 and 13.00 hrs.
    Toward the west: 08.30 and 15.30 hrs.
    Tunnels at Niederviller and Arzviller:
    Both directions: 06.30, 11.00 and 15.00 hrs.

The summit of the canal is at 900 feet above sea level.

Page 189

The Canal de l'Est (Southern Section) connects the Canal
Marne au Rhin with the river Saône at Corre. It passes
over the Vosges and attains a summit level of 1,200 feet
above sea level. It is 147 kilometres in length and there are
99 locks. There are two branches, one to Nancy and the
other to Epinal. There are no tunnels.

Index